A Fly Girl
Travel Tales of an Exotic British Airways Cabin Crew

Amanda Epe

A Fly Girl

Travel Tales of an Exotic British Airways Cabin Crew

by

Amanda Epe

LONDON

BLOSSOM BOOKS

First published in Great Britain by Blossom Books

This edition published by CompletelyNovel

A catalogue record of this book is available from the British Library

ISBN 9781849145589

Apart from the names mentioned in the Aboard chapter, my friend Angela in Kuala Lumpar and my Sisters Gloria and Julie, flight attendant Diana Greenway Neverson all other names that are in my story other than mentions of people in media have been changed and their original locations fictionalised to protect the identities of the people in this memoir.

"Many people, especially ignorant people, want to

punish you for speaking the truth, for being correct,

for being you.

Never apologize for being correct, or being years

ahead of your time.

If you're right and you know it, speak your mind.

Even if you are a minority of one, the truth is still the

truth."

~ Gandhi

For

A Fly Girl is for those of you who know the sky is your limit. Preye and Priscilla.

Table of Contents

Foreword

As far back as I can remember I always had a passion for writing as well as reading philosophy and poetry. It was one of my greatest joys as a child writing secret stories for myself and at school my stories were selected from the class and shared on the wall. As a young girl, I engaged in books and I didn't have any time or interest to play with dolls. I was noted for my calm and creative nature, however, my fun and adventurous side was unleashed when it came to arts, creativity and writing. During my secondary school years, I initiated a project and I transformed from a timid twelve year old girl to a bold journalist character. For the assignment, I interviewed the school Principal about his private affairs and used the article as the cover story. Such experiences made school unforgettable; I was enthralled by the power of creativity.

Listening to my father's stories as I sat cross-legged in the kitchen with my siblings had a profound effect on me and I craved more, likewise, at primary school sitting on the classroom carpet storytelling time was the highlight of my day. In my family as many African families do we were raised on true stories dating generations back, passed on from father to son and mother to daughter. I was captivated by these true stories more than the imaginary fables and other famous books for children. Yet being the fly on the wall I didn't tell my stories, I was the listener, the observer and the inquirer.

Eventually I began to write creatively. The experiences and satisfaction I got from writing personal essays outweighed the journalist writing I had done, biographic writing was helpful for me in understanding myself and society. Nicole Moore an author, poet, editor and independent publisher enabled many emerging and some established black and mixed race women writers in the U.K to have a voice through Shangwe anthologies. It was the first time I had published creative life writing. Unfortunately in Britain only less than one per cent of black writers are afforded the opportunity to be published, a report on poets by British Arts Council.

I had this Fly Girl story in me for far too long and in 2013, I was finally inspired to write it. I had to write this book because it was a period in my life that I wanted to go back to. It was time for me to analyse the past in order to prepare for my future. It was time for me to celebrate my journey because I had reached a spiritually serene space from which I could write. I share this story because I hope my readers can gain something or relate to my journey and perhaps reflect on changing times as society evolves in the record of history.

Chapter 1 Aboard

The first time I entered the iron tube cylinder my head was held high and my eyes worked in panoramic vision to capture my surroundings. I walked in single file pacifying the pep in my step in my brand spanking new and well fitting uniform. Only weeks earlier I had picked up my uniform from Uniform Stores; it was then that the circumference of my head, my shoulders and my neck were measured for a perfect fit. Donned in red, white and blue and a stiff straw hat perched on my head, I viewed the inside of the aircraft from a new perspective. We were at training, my peers also well groomed in navy blue and I stood huddled together at the top of the stairs of the Boeing 747. I listened intently to my trainer who took our group on the tour of the model, attentive in case she fired any questions my way. The aroma of detergent was strong as the service staffs had just sanitized the aeroplane. It appeared wide and spacious at that time of unfamiliarity. I entered the galley where we were split into groups to learn more about service and how to locate catering facilities. Most of what we were shown had been introduced to our batch of new recruits in training manuals and short films. We were now seeing it all for real. I had never been a lover of experimenting with food nor had I any industrial kitchen experience so I was overwhelmed with learning other cuisines. In a short space of time I had knowledge of world foods, diet preferences for medical or religious reasons and BA's equal opportunities policies with regard to choice on the menu. I learnt all about food from Kosher to Asian Vegetarian, to Vegan diets to meals for diabetics to specials.

I spent numerous afternoons training in the mock plane. I practiced emergency landings and ditching in case of catastrophes, and I had one of my own. It wasn't fun jumping out of the simulator whilst being watched by the trainers and the trainees especially being told to repeat things, when others didn't have to. The fear of failure in training added further pressure to my boot camp experience. I stood with clenched fists but not in a fighting mood. The technical training was not sinking in. I had techno phobia issues prior to my joining BA but the same vibrations of tension happened in classroom training too, even though studying airport codes, demographics of cities and national populations was far more interesting. I had been training for some weeks, and I expected it to become more relaxed as the training continued; however I was in need of a therapeutic massage at the end of most days. A major part of our training was Safety and Emergency Procedures, SEP, on air, on ground, in water and in fire; our main priority was saving lives. I studied much on health and was tried and tested, and equipped with first aid skills and I became a certified First Aider. Training to be a midwife in case of any early arrivals (which was part of the training), raised my blood pressure levels. British Airways standards where high, the brand was quality, and the training was intense. I was naive when I applied for the job. My desire for travelling and enjoyment had made me overlook the intense training involved. It hit me hard.

As a high flyer I took my journey to take pleasure in the world and life, aside from that, I took it to give; whether it was a sincere smile or superb service. As a fly girl I knew that the benefit of the work was appreciating all forms of life; the different classes, races and cultures I was to be exposed to. I believe that the recruitment officers noted this trait when they short listed me. It must have been evident that the depth of my soul was loving life and bonding with others. My passion was to fly. Each time I took a trip to Cranebank head office my soul danced at the prospect of global outreach presented to me in a fun and friendly package. I went on board to fulfil my dream at that particular stage in my life. I went on board to look outwardly to the world in my travels and this served as a catalyst for my writing aspirations.

I was elated when it became official that I was an employee of British Airways. I felt proud of my achievements and I was confident. I travelled to and from training on the underground and one day I was spotted by my cousin who worked on the underground.

Loud as ever his bellow mightier than the Tannoy, Patterson exclaimed, "Wow, look at you, you work for BA now, you represent!"

I was one of the few making us feel included as it was not the norm to see black women in a BA uniform. I did feel proud to wear the suit and to have immaculate nails and hair, although it was most annoying having to wear dreadful nylon tights and that brimmed hat on the underground. The tube passengers prepared me to get my practised smile right as they gazed at me on the Piccadilly line towards Heathrow and Hatton Cross and I had to smile back. One day a tall elder Englishman with sagging cheeks came to congratulate me as I waited on the platform, he was a frequent flyer with the corporation for an age, and was happy to see the changing faces over the years. I thanked him although deep inside I didn't enjoy drawing unnecessary attention. It was unlike me. The normal me had natural nail colour and hardly ever received a glance on the underground.

My first scheduled flight was delayed because I had to repeat part of my training. At least I had Bella retaking with me. The second time around we both passed with flying colours, and I received a new roster of different destinations. Whilst I was on training there was no rest for the ambitious to fly. In the evenings I had homework and revision and calls from demanding friends.

"Get me in." And, *"Can you get me an application form?"* They asked thinking my

employment would make it easier for them or that I could recommend a friend.

The recruitment process was long, almost half a year from applying to being given a start date. Some friends thought my work was praiseworthy and asked if they could partner in business ventures of international trade, other people called me a glorified waitress. Getting employed by BA got people in my community talking about me.

"British Airways standards have dropped, they take anyone these days," was an unexpected insult from a black sister who must have thought that black was synonymous with inferior. She obviously didn't believe that black could represent.

To represent I had to be uniformed as an equal to my peers, this meant in both my behaviour and appearance. When in uniform we needed certain decorum, a standard. In public we were prohibited from eating and drinking, neither could smokers smoke in non designated areas. In my attempt to assimilate and blend in with the other ladies my hair was my first priority. Before working for the airline I experimented with natural hair after a decade of relaxers and curly perms. I was enjoying my kinky afro, curls and waves as well as African hairstyles using thread. However, wearing an African high crowned style or my large chic afro and trying to fit a hat on top, was a task unworthy of a try so to fit in, I became a regular customer of an elite black hair salon and restarted the chemical process once again so that

I could wear my hair in a straight style or in a bun at the nape like most other employees.

Cohorts of black sisters went before me and a few were employed during the period I was. I was following in their footsteps in the quest to venture the world. In my research (I wanted to find out about their journeys), I interviewed Diana Aandi Greenway Neverson who had done long service in the airline as a cabin crew flight attendant. She was an example that dreams come true. In the sixties era it was unheard of for black women to be employed by the airline, but as a child she had a dream to be a flyer. Diana Neverson started her career as a mature woman, previously selection criteria was that the corporation did not hire women over the age of 36. Diana had a wealth of interesting stories to share and most remarkable and humanitarian was her dream flight to Orlando where she served 192 ill and disabled children. She was inspired by them as they overcame their challenges and enjoyed life. More recently Diana has ventured into pilot training, an interest associated with few women. Her story is an example of being unstoppable despite age, gender and race barriers.

In 1958 Ruth Carol Taylor was the 1st African-American flight stewardess. In the 1960's both in the UK and in the USA, civil rights movements and protests took place so that people of colour could be employed in work other than menial jobs. There were major protests in Britain and America on black employment matters, such as Paul Stephenson leading a bus boycott in Bristol in 1963 simultaneously with the Martin Luther King Jnr movement.

Fifty years on from civil rights movements, I started to write and record the celebrations and challenges of employment as an exotic British Airways flight stewardess. My journeys document memorable destinations and recall the highs and lows in my Fly Girl mission. Embarking on a life as a globe trotter in my quest to connect with citizens of the world and encounter new terrains had opened my mind beyond the box. In that solitary confinement of an aircraft, breathing the same recycled oxygen, I met and engaged with people from all walks of life. Striking conversations with strangers in economy class or in the upgraded spacious seats and looking out for passenger safety was to connect to humanity, and to bond as one family in the sky. Studying global cultures, and faiths, histories and geographies was the beginning of the journey. I penned my places of interest and learning experiences. I was ready to be a student of life so sit back, relax and ravel in my world, and enjoy the flights.

Chapter 2 Ascending

"Chicken or beef Sir/Madam? Chicken or beef?" repeated every minute with a programmed smile at 33,000 feet. This was my routine as I prepared for adventures to explore the world journaling my travels. I counted my blessings as to be fortunate enough to be selected to travel the world and board in five star hotels and meet the most fascinating people, some well known and others unsung heroes and heroines. It was a privilege to lodge in luxury and cover all corners of the globe. I hailed from a quintessential marginalised migrant family background that had rarely enjoyed air travel; however, through my work as a fly girl, I landed in many territories that were virgin to me.

Fifty shades darker than the rest, I was. Scarlet stained collagen free lips and fully masked in foundation – that was the policy to get the job done - appearance mattered! On duty I was like a doll my face the colours of a paint pallet with shades of grey, blue, and red. Although having grown up in Britain, my genetic makeup which was different to the indigenous population disturbed some of the team members I worked with: race mattered!

The corporation changed gradually and I was part of new batches of ethnic minorities being recruited at that particular time. In the late nineties speakers of the Yoruba language were called to apply to the airline, it was also a time when the corporation reinvented itself with ethnic livery. In my twenties I had a dream to fly and I joined the airline to accomplish that dream. Other black women I had spoken to also had dreams, many followed their childhood dream to work as a stewardess, and worked hard to achieve this. When I decided to apply for a job in the airline industry, I knew that we as black women were and are, a minority in various industries of employment. However, I also knew that times had changed from the days of rejection in the airlines if you were over thirty six, unattractive, married, on the rounder side, or black. Libbie Escolme Schmidt describes the then preferred type representing British Airways in her book *Glamour in the Skies,* as young, attractive and European. After several applications to various airlines, being shortlisted, under going interview tasks, psychometric testing, selection processes and back to back rejections, I finally hit the jackpot. I was not only employed as crew member of the national carrier but I felt victorious as I had been posted to long haul flights and that was my ideal.

Rejection after rejection, I picked myself up, dusted myself off and tried again; such was my pillar of faith and strength. My family saw faith in me, but ultimately I had faith in myself and it paid off. On my first flight, I pinched myself as I realised that after years of striving I was now a black ambassador of Britain. I realised that, if one believes in their destinies and dreams with undying faith, and actively pursues these dreams, ultimately they manifest.

Chapter 3 Americana

Flight JFK

I woke up soaked in sweat from a sleepless night, ready for the big day; my first flight destined to New York. I was fused with excitement and trepidation, the fear of the purser- a senior team member of the crew in each service section of the aircraft- doing my first in flight assessment form worked up my adrenalin. I was very excited, as the big apple was full of entertainment and offered more than what I could bite. It had this effect on many young Londoners' and particularly those who loved the whole popular culture of African American entertainment. It was the city that as a teenager my siblings and I fantasised about, the images of black people in media and the music had consistently been stateside. From Hollywood movies to programmes such as *The Cosby Show* in the 80s my friends and I identified with what was then known as Black Americans, they were our role models. The city was also notorious for gun crime and gang culture and visions of energetic young to withered black men hustling in the streets. These were the images of New York City that resonated with me. Cop programmes of the 70's such as Starsky and Hutch always depicted a young black male being arrested in a drug raid, and the impression given was that all youth had guns.

As an avid follower of the old skool rap music, I was educated on the underground stories out of New York, the battles from the communities from uptown, the rap and break-dance competitions between the boroughs of Bronx, Brooklyn and Queens. The pictures painted from the tales of the underground musical poets always spun a story of hardship, from the school of hardknox to the stage of celebrated stardom of rapping. Dark derelict buildings surrounded with groups of the underclass huddled together making raps, plans and sharing codes of behaviour in the hoods. It was grim yet enticing, the street life showed life and set the trends for large proportions of western black youth all over the Northern hemisphere. And it was here that so many of my young friends wanted to and some did, migrate. Firstly, they experimented with summer vacation jobs of Camp America, whilst secretly hoping to chance across fame and the road to stardom, as that is what America offered in its media portrayal. One friend followed the footsteps of a successful U.K born rapper *Monie Love* a young lady in the 90's who went on to make it big time in the U.S.A, although he says he had amazing experiences unfortunately for him he could not sign record deals and his dream was shattered. Another friend became a popular radio host; the dream that ended for her in the U.K became a reality in America. It was these stories of opportunities that made my eyes twinkle at the thought of U.S.A. And after years of watching soaps and shows from across the Atlantic, my mind was preoccupied with all things American, and therefore for me it was always the preferred destination.

On my first ever visit across the pond, a trip prior to working as a crew member; on arrival I reflected on the years of watching programmes of darkness and violence and I had to question what was it that enticed me to be a follower of *I Love New York* and *New York, New York* chants. I had grown out of the teenage phase of loving rap music but not with the love for the States. As I toured, retoured and detoured inch by inch the city grew smaller in my mind. The New Yorkers were ecstatic as conversationalists, food and shopping malls were grand and appealing but the bubble had burst, and if I convinced myself that this wasn't true, the expressions on public faces and the discussions with people confirmed that many bubbles had been burst. I loved studying the sense of paranoia on most passengers' crumpled foreheads on the underground network system. The trains made the horrific screeching noise and the cold metallic hard seats made you want to get off sooner other than later. I did the typical tourist things of downtown sightseeing at the statue of Liberty. I hung around Time Square from dawn to dusk, and killed the calories from the oversized meals by climbing. It was an experience climbing the twin towers of the World Trade Centre with two pursuing stockbroker immigrants from Barbados. It was the highlight of the day tour hanging around with these two well-groomed men the black version of Lauren and Hardy. Little Lauren was ever so polite and pitching his intention for courtship whilst homeboy Hardy bellowed his obnoxious comments all over the town, embarrassing his colleague.

"Where did you get to know these shorties?" he kept asking his friend, who tried to stop him using the term. I found the pair hilarious, but Lauren blushed obviously flustered by the words and behaviours of his co-worker. Each profanity or gesture from his colleague made the blood rush to Lauren's cheeks transforming his yellowy complexion.

"I am sorry he is calling you shorti." he said.

"You don't need to apologise for him."

"Honestly he can be so embarrassing at times, we just work together."

"So tell me about your work." I tried to make Lauren feel relaxed and less agitated by his peer.

We reached the top of the twin towers and were ready for a bite to eat, when Hardy apologised to the group and announced that nature called, forgetting or oblivious to the fact that women were in his presence he went to the corner and released himself, his waste forming into a little frothy puddle amidst the tourists. At that point Lauren thought all his chances were blown and was thrown off balance suggesting that we should descend and make our way back home. The high wind was tossing my bone straight relaxed hair out of style; at that time my hair was a priority; so I agreed with Lauren.

Continuing and going beyond the tourist mode, my venture took me to no go areas and into the ghetto, to what was called The Projects. Friends of friends had led me to see and meet families who could tell me their experiences of survival and poverty in the first world of America. That holiday showed me that all that glitters is not gold; The U.S had a large underclass of African Americans, and the type of suffering I saw, made America lose its glitzy appeal. Still, I was excited to be heading back to New York on my first flight working with BA. It was mid autumn and I had packed jeans and sweaters, for the back-to-back night stops. The most exciting thing was that my dear sister Gloria had moved to US and was living in New York at that time. I would have had my initiation with the crew at the bar with a few rounds of drinks on my first night with the Union Jack family had I not arranged to meet my sister who was coming down from Queens to see me in Manhattan. I checked into my room admiring the plush surroundings and dived into the shower, although lethargic, I tried to recharge myself, it had been a long day following a long sleepless night, a long and busy flight and now the time zone was at least five hours behind GMT. I ordered room service and sipped cheerfully on some wine whilst I made calls to my family back home, I was in my element and still feeling like I was flying high. On my first night I was too happy to sleep.

The next morning I managed to make it to breakfast with the crew, but declined any shopping trip or excursion as Gloria and I had made plans plus my intention was to visit friends. As I started making my way around and asking for directions I saw the similarities between the residents of London and New York, the rat race. On my initial trip I was so in awe of the US and the happy smiley people who acknowledged each other with a greeting that it escaped me to notice the pace of the place, or listen to the fellow New Yorkers who told it as it was. But now I was not on holiday, not touring and looking for souvenirs and gifts but I was utilising my down route time to get to specific destinations. I had the underground maps but still wanted the human contact to ask, to speak and to connect with global citizens. The responses were abrupt or agitated, perhaps they didn't want to be disturbed or they didn't know the directions but it wasn't the warmth of the Americans I previously had encounters with. I decided to rely on myself but still dared to ask the do not approach faces when I couldn't make head or tail of my map. When I arrived in Queens and was busy shopping around I heard someone call my name, faintly

"Amanda..."

It was surreal as if I was in my local town centre, where at least I could account for my popularity, unlike here where I had only spent a vacation. I was with Gloria and we had been spotted by a friend of hers who immediately knew she was my sister from the resemblance, and he had also heard about me. The friends, the lunch and all the social interaction made me feel included and had me forgetting that I was on assignment and in between an extended break period. In such events where one travels, meets family and friends, engages with activities and community, and the environment feels familiar the world seems smaller. New York could be home. This home was now my sister's home, also British born and bred, but now a New Yorker. My pride and joy, the red, white and majorly blue uniform was hanging in my room in Manhattan along with my hat placed carefully in its hat box, I thought for a minute, *wherever I place my hat that's my home.* The city was much like the city I was born and raised in and it was extremely diverse, Brooklyn borough like the borough of Brent had African-Caribbean shopping centres galore. It was just like home, with that exciting edge, my sister had made it her home, and in my heart of hearts I may have also wanted to. This was the city that inspired me to be A Fly Girl; the hip hop culture coined the term fly girl to define a girl woman who was involved in rap, the street community, and was stylish and admirable. I saw myself as a *rapoet*, someone who combines poetry with the rhyme set of the rap genre, and I also loved to reach out to people in the community. It was this city that made the expression of a Fly Girl literal on my first working flight, although in my teens I organised a hip hop dance fundraiser for Great Ormond Street Hospital, and the fly girl archetype was introduced.

Back at the hotel as I boarded the bus and waved goodbye to my sister the crew remarked at our resemblance and then questioned me about her, if and why she lived in the USA. My response then as is now was of words to the effect that: the heart and the head determine the place of the home.

On another trip to Queens I went to the African American centre to visit a friend and pick up a few bits of their abundant variety of hair cosmetics. I shopped around reading the labels of products and then I stopped to skim through a beauty magazine. A shopper spoke and startled me "Hey babe, what are you going to do with your hair?"

"Not sure on the look yet, wow there's so many styles to choose from."

"This one will suit you." She pointed at a style whilst peering over the magazine I held

"I do like it too, but I will need something conventional for work."

"I love your accent, where you from?"

"London, England..."

"It's my dream to go to Europe, and see the queen, and oh yer Buckingham Palace"

The conversation went on about the similarities, differences between USA and U.K, the likes and dislikes and the haves and have not's, with a baby or cutie dropped every now and then into sentences. It was nice to engage deeply with a stranger, other than the average two sentence conversation. I always thought that American's where chatty, but I really wasn't expecting to make a friend. The shopper gathered that I was a little distant or reserved English, and questioned me further. "Are you in a relationship?" I was not about to bare my soul to a stranger shopper. As I contemplated her question she boldly said "I am attracted to you and would like to get to know you more."

I was taken aback. I had never been clued up on when opposites were attracted to me. If a man who was interested in me didn't clearly express his interest, I couldn't guess. Furthermore I wouldn't expect a woman to chat me up, especially as we were not in Greenwich Village. As a tourist on my first trip in New York I had wandered through the village a tourist attraction vicinity and it was the first time in public had I seen LGBT in the black community, and this was the first time a woman hit on me, I was not totally shocked as I was aware of diverse sexual orientations there but it was a strange experience. In the 90s, in the black community in Britain, it was rare to hear a black person openly state that they were gay. It was an era when homophobia in the black community was so high such that a song by a popular artist Buju Banton which had lyrics about violence towards homosexuals was a hit.

But in an ordinary shopping district in Queens this lady had the confidence to express her interest in me. Britain and America were not that similar. I then wondered; if this African-American

31

lady was in Britain would she be as daring as to state her sexual orientation as boldly as she did? As the Statue of Liberty stands tall, it states that America is evidently the free world.

Flight SFO

"Cabin crew doors to manual and cross check," the pilot announced. Sarah the non stop pecker and picker of flight nibbles and I smiled at each other as we landed from a long eleven hour flight, most of which we had been on our feet shuffling between excitable tourists, and families taking screaming children on Easter breaks. I hadn't slept up in the crew rest bunks, turbulence always seemed to happen when it was my time to rest and before I could shut my eyes I was making my way back from the tail of the aircraft to prepare the breakfast service. I was tired even before I got to work the day before.

I travelled to Heathrow all the way from my apartment in central London on the tube. I was flustered with my hat fixed firmly on my head, handbag hanging of my shoulder, hatbox in my left hand and right hand clasping my hand luggage. I stood my main suitcase up against the panel by the doors of the train. The first line I took there was not a seat in sight as all the city workers were squeezed together in the rush hour. Transferring to the Piccadilly line was the saving grace, after lugging my luggage up and down the escalators, with damp underarms, I eventually found a seat. Of all the handsome hunks who normally gave me the wanted attention on the underground, at rush hour there was not even one insight to help a damsel in distress, but although feeling morose if my eye caught another passenger, I would just smile in that uniform. Arriving at the Compass Centre for briefing I knew I had to be a superwoman and summon up strength for the long voyage to San Francisco.

Just before the flight landed I topped up my lips with fresh ruby red lipstick. With both my baby toes throbbing, I changed back into my high navy court shoes from the flat loafers I wore for the in service. As the passengers disembarked I tried to appear wide awake as I smiled and wished them a pleasant day. I still had to face the start of the day as it was eight hours behind GMT. It was not an occupation for the faint hearted, under the glamorous appearance of service with a smile; at the end of most flights the team and I were shattered. It became clear to me why many of the veteran crew were reluctant to accompany me on excursions when I first joined the crew a diehard diva, eager to explore cities. My older colleagues had been there bought the t-shirt, postcards and paraphernalia and understandably had no desire to do it again and again. However, at that time when I had made requests and had been rejected back-to-back, my thoughts were; *it's probably because I am black and they can't relate to me.* I made things personal and my thoughts left me feeling despondent. But if I am honest I know that had I stayed in the job for years and if a new member of staff were to ask me to trek along with them to new ventures, I too would have made that new person feel dejected as my priority would be to get my beauty sleep back and look after self.

The striking city of San Francisco, its hilly scenery and Victorian architecture, kissed with the bright and bearing sunshine and cool breeze released my tensions. It was a wide and populated city and appeared very diverse in race and culture. I skimmed through tourist brochure material to look for landmarks and popular hotspots. On arrival some of the crew arranged for us to have dinner on the waterfront where I saw tipsy tourists from all over the world indulge in fine fish dishes and pricey wine. It was presumably a city of bliss by the look of the terrain, the streetscapes adorned by green and concrete mounts, and the colourful houses and buildings of Spanish design were breath-taking. As I captured the layout of my surroundings I observed that the city boasted wealth. It was evident that the masses of visitors further boosted the cities income. In the evening I wandered amidst rows of expensive boutiques. I couldn't do any more than window shop.

On the next day feeling more refreshed my colleagues and I made our way to an excursion to the Golden Gate Bridge. The walk was an adventure compared to the new hobby I acquired of drinking as a social event. Taking in the panoramic views from the bridge of clear skylines and the backdrop of the city was therapeutic. On that occasion, I felt fearless on the Grandeurs Bridge which was 220 feet above the sea. Perhaps the power of the waters had calmed me, as I usually found being suspended on a bridge an unpleasant and body trembling experience. Knowing that it was built in 1933 and was over sixty years was a little worrying, but the lively Liverpudlian presence of Sarah pacified me. I could see why it was one of the most photographed bridges in the world and one of the wonders of the modern world as described by American Society of Civil Engineers. I had made it to San Francisco and across America's main attraction and it was well worth the tourist ticket price for the treasured memory.

I also made an outing to the Alcatraz Federal Penitentiary, to view the former prison of America's worst criminals and murderers. It was serene travelling by ferry from Pier 41 at Fisherman's Wharf, no turbulence until arrival. I could sense the ills whilst on the Alcatraz Island, and looking at the photographs of the notorious criminals sent shivers down my spine. Leading up to this tour our bigoted tour guide may have tried to build the momentum to visiting a city which he described as home to the worst of mankind. We had taken the cable cars and were ticking off all to do's and see places. One of the tour guides spat out his verbal diarrhoea as he went on elaborating that the city has the worst kind of people: *Blacks and gays.* In the late 90's people were not politically correct and this man lacked foresight. I guess he would not have imagined that in exactly ten years a partially black man would be elected president of his country. The speaker had no regard for me as a black tourist on the bus, he reiterated facts about the down and out areas where the black community live and stereotyped them as all being involved with crime. This was definitely not a guided history tour, as he had missed the crucial point that many African Americans had laboured extensively in this city, and travelled from the Northeast and the South to contribute their specialist skills to the shipping industry. African-Caribbean, Cape-Verde, West African seamen had also assisted in the marine trade of San Francisco. It was of no importance to dwell on the ignorance of this particular man yet it seemed all too often that in America, the race card was played unfairly and the consequence of that was an out pour of rage from the marginalised inhabitants of the city.

All in all I still had admiration for the landscapes of sunny San Fran, the contrast of the delicate warmth and cool breeze aided my morning exercise on the steep inclines as I walked around for the rest of the days spent there. I even managed to shop in the pricey stores as prices were incredibly slashed in the sales. I found that every time I started a conversation with staff, my British accent and particularly being a Black British seemed to intrigue my audience. It was the time when the pop band Spice Girls where reigning and I ordered my food, thinking the staff couldn't detect my order. I repeated the order several times, only to be told that they loved my intonation and I was asked if I was from the same region as Mel B as I sounded just like her, and only her from the group. I guess this is not much different from saying West Coast sound like East Coast; it was their fascination of European African Diaspora.

Flight LAX

I was lied to, and so many others were lied to by the British singer Albert Hammond in his song, *It Never Rains in Southern California.* I believed Los Angeles was a sunshine city 24/7 just as Hammond sang. If not for the exposure through rap music, my shock from my experiences in this city would have been more severe. Growing up listening to stateside rap had intensified my interest in the West Coast life style of African Americans'. Mainstream Hollywood alone was not sufficient enough for a fly girl like me to be fully engaged. I needed to relate with and compare the lives of African Diaspora's who lived in Western white worlds, whether it was in the U.K, mainland Europe or the USA. As a loyal listener to BBC Radio DJ Tim Westwood from the late 80' to 90's I was introduced to underground stars and the underground life. It was impossible to believe that this same city of wealth and celebrities also spun tales of guns and violence in disadvantaged neighbourhoods. At that time of my life I transited from learning from the underground media the real life of a large proportion of the black community, to a strong detest of the rap music and culture. With bands like NWA (Nigga's With Attitude) whose rap narrated life on the street and blatantly revealed their sexual exploits in a profane and chauvinistic manner, I opted out of my long term love affair with and intimacy of hip hop. It was a painful divorce as my original relationship with rap music was totally positive; as a teen the group Public Enemy and the likes of KRS1 were my educators and empowered many of us youth in the U.K by teaching us important and political lessons. As the years progressed gradually my interest waned as the consciousness disappeared and capitalism got the better of the hip hop culture. I realised that a number of artists were there for a quick buck and popularisation. In retrospect, it was also necessary to hear from the less conscious rappers, they had stories of their lives in America and it was essential that the world heard their stories of crime and rage, whether we liked it or not. The rappers stories were not regarded as important unlike the coverage of personalities in superficial Hollywood. Conceivably the music may have enticed its idolizing fans to belong to gangs; but I believe telling the gang style life stories wasn't the root of the gang culture, but rather the indifferent negligent attitude of the government towards these communities.

"May I have 300 US dollars please?" I asked smiling whilst handing in my gold card.

"Wow, this is amazing, you sound just like Oprah" she replied gazing into my eyes in awe. I was now pondering if in all my travels I was beginning to imitate the American intonation, but this was not a generic accent I only sounded like Oprah; I had to read between the lines. The remaining crew who were also queuing up at the concierge for cash withdrawals waited patiently as the receptionist babbled on.

"Oprah is amazing, she speaks so articulately, and I have never heard a black women speak like her."

Well obviously this garrulous woman had not been listening, perhaps only to herself! Her words fell on deaf ears. Racial comments tend to embarrass or make people blush. Of all the crew, only one member who was of German-Jewish origin openly said to me that the lady's comments had racist implications. I was in cloud nine in LA and those types of shallow comments were not going to put me down. They only exposed the ignorance I had already encountered in some of my travels. Many people made offensive remarks unintentionally, or sometimes people were offensive because they believed the lies and stereotypes. To travel, integrate and investigate helped to expose the lies I had been told. Martina the hops and malt expert, and I had made friends as we worked on the flight into Los Angeles. The two of us had planned our exciting excursions in LA. Still on GMT time and after a lengthy flight we were rearing to go on a foray before we took a rest. Welcome to Los Angeles, it was going to be a blast. Hollywood movies like *Boys in the hood* had put the spotlight on this city of action and Martina and I planned on getting about like girls in the hood.

Unlike its sister city New York, Los Angeles metro transportation system was not as advanced. Los Angeles was a car friendly metropolis. The metro had only been in operation since 1990. We used a combination of the metro rail and metro buses to move around. Our first stop was the Paul Getty Art

Centre, a spacious state of art design that had only recently been opened to the public. The site spread across 24 acres of land in the Getty Museum on the Santa Monica Mountains; the campus incorporated a picturesque sculptured garden, research institute and municipal buildings. Mass collections were displayed of drawings, paintings, sculptures and other fascinating arts that to see it all we had to spend the whole day.

At lunch Martina introduced me to the benefits of lager. She insisted that that hops gave Germans their good build. My palette appreciated the taste of lager which was new to me as I was more accustomed to fermented fruit wine. We sat on the terrace and enjoyed the freshly baked potatoes with lemon squeezed salad, lots of brew and one another's company. We resumed our tour of the Art Centre after lunch. I spent a fair amount of time feeling the works of arts from American and European artefacts however; I felt the art collection was not representative of the country's multiple ethnicities. Sometime during the afternoon Martina and I separated in the maze and could not relocate each other. It was at the time when mobile phones weren't a necessity neither was roaming. For that period of solitude as I continued viewing the display, I felt a connection to a divine source. I listened to my inner voice and felt gratitude for my life and encounters with people. Later I travelled back to the hotel alone. Martina and I met later on that evening. We were both unnerved by the experience of travelling alone at night in the unfamiliar city of Los Angeles. We counted our blessings for getting back to the hotel safely.

I was blessed to also have a friend of a friend living in Los Angeles who took precious time out to chauffer me around in the evening after his long working day. I got a guided tour of Beverly Hills and I got to see how the other quarter lived. I saw oversized mansions and pristine palaces mounted up on highland for the dreamers to look up to, in hope. We drove along Rodeo Road to see how the residents of Beverly Hills shopped. The price tags were jaw dropping. I connected with the rich and famous; I stood on Patti La Belle's star engraved on the pavements of star names. Hollywood and the bright lights were amazing; I was a fly girl that reached for the stars on the ground, and I was a star in my own right.

Transiting through downtown Los Angeles by night was far from amazing. I was returning back to the hotel after a South Central independent tour experiencing, *The hood*. I ventured through notorious areas such as Inglewood and Compton, which were a sharp contrast to the glitz and glamour I just experienced. As I passed through these neighbourhoods alone on a deserted bus, as only the severely disadvantaged used buses, I felt anxiety start to creep up in me. I then realised that I had missed my stop and hence lost my connection as I had got off the bus a little too late. I started to wonder around looking for a land mark I could recognise, but all the roads looked the same to me. As I walked back and forth without making progress I began to feel knots in my stomach and my heart started to pound. I began to feel paranoid that people would know I was a stranger in the neighbourhood and maybe I was wearing the wrong colours. I certainly had missed taking lessons for a rough guide to the ghetto.

I should have taken note from rapper Ice Cube; he waxed lyrical on in the track *How to Survive in South Central*. He said; *make sure you are back before dark in Compton*. It was a warning to adhere to, so was his guidance, *don't trust anyone*. To my relief, I spotted two men in uniform, one burly the other tall, patrolling the streets and felt that luck was on my side, I hurriedly approached them. I spoke to the Los Angeles Police officers as I tried to locate which direction I needed to be going in order to get back to the hotel. Both of the LAPD constables looked at me as if I was speaking gibberish. Slowly and clearly I repeated myself but to no effect. So I showed them the map of my destination. I then realised that they were just redundant men in uniform with no pity for a vulnerable lady lost and alone in the middle of the night. I gave up on them and decided I had to find my way out. I put on what I hoped was a gangster face so as to look as if I was from the hood. Ice Cube had rapped the truth about trusting no one. For the rest of the journey I used my own judgement, and I had a consoling thought that just like my own fear maybe the police officers could have been fearful of me too, as survival rule number one of the people in that community seemed to be was *get yourself a gun*.

As Martina and I moved around the city; it became evident that an unofficial apartheid system existed in LA. There was a form of colour coding. If it wasn't the colours of gangs with their red or blue bandannas, it was the shades of skin tone; each community had their territory; African-American, European or Hispanic populations. As we ventured deeper into the ethnic minority communities the areas looked more impoverished, it was no surprise to me as Ice Cube had painted this picture and reported in his lyrics; *there are no blondes as in the movies*. At least my dark haired German-Jewish friend blended in that respect, yet understandably she also felt uncomfortable as the only white person on public transport as we weaved into African American neighbourhoods. Perhaps if Martina the lover of beer was to hold a can of *Forty*, the brew street boys drank, then she would have fitted in well.

Both the bright and the dark side of the city was a grand experience. All kinds of people were attracted to Los Angeles as the city in which to make a break. Crossing the road in Beverly Hills one afternoon a young lady and I became acquainted. Perhaps we both could see we derived from the same source. She had left a small South Eastern town in Nigeria to head for the hills, although she was a cleaner she shared with me her dream that she would be among the stars one day, and like me standing on star paved grounds she already was. That was Los Angeles it allowed everyone to dream.

Flight MIA

"Welcome to Miami" Marie sang with her permanent smile sitting widely across her face. She unlike the rest of the crew had reserved some energy after the long flight. She dashed to customs and immigration eager to get to the action the city had to offer. As we disembarked the aircraft and entered the airport the mood of the Boeing 777 staff changed. It was as if a new leash of life was thrust upon us. The ambience of the city was energizing; none of the usual groans of tiredness or murmurs of *been here before* were heard. I awakened to a scenic airport, bright and airy from the inside and outside view too. I noticed the large welcoming signs in many languages, paying particular attention to English as Spanish writing was very bold and dominant, followed by French. The arrivals area was very large and colourful and welcoming.

It was great to have Marie the hostess wannabe mistress as company as she was full of vitality and positivity. We worked together inbound and synchronised our duties so much that the uniformed smile became authentic and unstoppable. Passengers commented on us as we served in adjacent aisles, complimenting us on the aura we were spreading and said we were boosting their holiday frame of mind, many of the passengers were British families taking their children to Disney in Orlando.

Time was of the essence and Maria and I made the most of this our first visit to Miami. The weather facilitated our agenda. Although it was officially summer, the air was fresh and the sky an aqua blue. In the municipal area the roads were wide and clean. It was an attractive city in its natural beauty and climate, notwithstanding the manmade cityscape views.

Over the months I had gained so much weight I was hardly recognisable from the ideal body mass index, BMI I was when recruited. I had been weighed and measured for short listing procedures and was a perfect 10 borderline size 12, the ideal for my body frame. I was happy with my weight and my toned appearance which added to my confidence when I started the job. Three months into the job the weight started piling on, however I didn't pay the matter any regard. But in Miami about eight months after I joined, I asked myself who the person in the mirror was. It couldn't be me. There was no chance for me to be a beach babe in a bikini. I was squeezing myself tight into a size 12 and I should have been wearing a size 14. I had never been fat and so I was caught unaware when I finally decided to take note of what I saw in the mirror. What had happened?   It was probably the result of over indulgence of buying duty free products on every return flight, not one but two or three or whatever the limit of alcohol allowance was. Furthermore, as we arrived to our destinations the crew *moi* included, would scurry and empty the passenger drinks bars of any remaining stock. This was our reward and for our personal pleasures. Most of the small shots and wines we drank on the coach to the hotel, and still on arrival at the hotel we purchased more for dinner at restaurants. I had in a short time acquired an appreciation of different alcoholic beverages from regions all over the world, and was becoming an expert on brands and booze. In my earlier days I was judgemental of crew's habit of downing drinks at any opportunity, but before long it was a case of you can't beat them join them. Not that drinking was anything new to me. I had already been indoctrinated into the culture of excessive drinking as a college student, but as a crew member, alcohol was as abundant as tap water.

Maria who had been recruited a few months after me was still new and excited, and she brought that excitement back to me. She injected me with a fresh dose of energy and enjoyment, without alcohol. We declined the crew booze up in the bar that evening and went on a tour; two lively ladies hit the town running. After an unforgettable night out I was hoping to gain some beauty sleep, by lying in for a while. But not with Maria, my wakeup call had been turned off, but she put it on again by calling me early the next morning to tell me she was going for a swim.

"You go girl," I said suggesting that she should leave me out. The sun was out and it was best to make the most of the day, but I had slowly lost all my energy, the new me was a young woman drained of vitality. It was good whilst travelling to eat out and indulge in delicacies though too much of anything wasn't good, and I couldn't do what I knew was good for me, exercise. Somehow before brunch Maria persuaded me to play a round of tennis. It was both a fun and frustrating game as she made me run for that ball, back and forth and only a few times was I able to whack it back. The game made me realize what I had been missing and what I had recently lost; my fitness.

During the day we ventured out into town for shopping and sightseeing and male bird watching. Maria was even able to talk to the birds, using her fluency in her mother tongue Portuguese. Hailing from an African Portuguese colony she connected with the Portuguese and Spanish speakers going about their daily business. She was becoming a good friend as we had previously worked together on another trip and I was pleased to have travelled with her to the glorious city of Miami. Her Latin language skills and Latino appearance helped as she asked for directions amongst mostly Cuban communities.

"Here is one for you" she said as she pointed out to an athletic young man.

Looking back I see how I spat opportunities out to meet and flirt with attractive young men. Unlike Maria's energy and enthusiasm for meeting young men I was responsible for sexual repulsion to keep up the good girl persona. It was bad enough drinking excessively, as a traditional African girl to chase a man was a deadly sin. But there was another truth to be told as to why there was no way I could get close to any man at the time. Soon after I joined the airline I developed a condition that was unladylike and far from becoming. As far as I believed, my type of women had to be prim and dolled up, and generally the golden rule in my book was that proper women don't let off wind. But I was letting off every other minute discreetly of course, except in the comfort of my hotel room all alone when I could let off with a big bang. Before joining the airline I was a proper woman and I hardly farted, but after I started spending half my life in the air, letting off wind became my new illness. So I let Maria point out the men she sought for me but deep inside I knew I had an embarrassing condition that I was not about to disclose or expose to anyone.

We spent a good stretch of the day chilling at the sandy seashore with its transparent waters. Maria had planned to top up her tan lying in her bikini on South Beach, but was enticed into playing volleyball by some local lads. It was double exercise for me, and at the end of it I saw how much I could really do in a day when I set my mind to really living and making use of the moment. By night we had met with the cabin crew boys who wanted to eat and chill out with us. The variety of restaurants on the sea front was alluring with cuisines and chilled cocktails and rum punches from Caribbean and South America, alongside grooves of Reggae, Meringue, Zouk and dance music. It was a tropical ambiance that recharged my draining batteries, connecting with the vibrant Jamaican men tourists and newly arrived migrants of the Islands not far off. I also had to do my usual routine of shopping just to purchase an item from every city. It felt a bit like being in Britain on hearing so many accents similar to those from home. I even connected with a few British born Caribbean sisters, the new Americans.

Miami was a taste of paradise. I became acquainted to the city through the television series Miami Vice. Unlike in LA I didn't venture into disadvantaged communities, or search for the hip hop world. The hip hop world was apparent around me, in terms of the language, fashion and body gestures. Miami had already gained the world's attention through their rap music with the controversial songs of groups such as *2 Live Crew*. Their music exploited women sexually, with the lyrics and video imagery and I didn't want to witness this culture of sexualisation in music at the clubs. I enjoyed the beauty of Miami, the bass and exhilarating beats was enough to satisfy me without being offended sexually.

I loved the West Coast as much as Miami and they both were more memorable voyages in comparison to other mid and East Stateside trips and the enchanted landscapes of calm Canada. Although on one trip I met and I hung out with my brother and other friends in Boston, it was lodging in the hotel with six foot plus, tall dark and handsome top basket ball players, the Boston Celtics that made that trip memorable. On the flight to Boston there was also a stimulating passenger who rang for my attention persistently and I was ready to fully attend to him in his seat at 28E. "*Je peux t'aider?*" I conversed in the language of love as I had already established much about him, his multi-linguist and other skills. This passenger got my sincerest smile of all my seven million smiles acted or actual. It was this type of affinity that made flights exciting and these customer interactions registered in my mind.

I had connected to American people and awakened from the American dream. I grew up to associate culturally with African Americans and their rap culture, yet when I spoke to African Americans I discovered that there were many differences as well as similarities between us. I grew up in a suburban area with predominately English families and a few neighbours of Asian and Caribbean backgrounds, but mostly in the states ethnic communities lived separately. I could relate to struggles as a black person in the west but not to the separatist street life of the rappers that had previously interested me. The street was out of bound for me as a teenager and the constructed concept of black popular culture of urban youth was not relevant to me. From my travels I realised it was superficial to attempt to claim that identity. Maybe I had grown up, I still loved the entertainment world America offered, but there was more to explore than only and all things American. As a people I recognised the similarities we shared across the pond, although we had many nuances, but the dream of an American utopia was over for me.

The USA although vastly segregated was nonetheless in many cities a massive melting pot of emulsifying flavours. I love to add flavour, it is this flavour sweet as cinnamon and fiery as ginger that makes human beings a magnificent race, and as the Jamaican motto says *out of many one people*. I once thought I had landed in the heart of Africa as all the airport staffs in Washington DC were African American; the US is the solely macro multi-racial land with echoes of the African voice. I had taken large bites many times from the big apple. My appetite of America had been satisfied. But as A Fly Girl, I had to keep moving beyond the America's in which I had the Western connection with and taste the spices of magical Arabia.

Chapter 4 Arabiana

Flight KWI

It was preparation for Armageddon, the briefing meeting was the longest that I had experienced. Gloom was written in capital letters across the faces of the team ready to take off for the Kuwaiti State. The subdued energy flowed from one to another, but it did not affect me, it was my first trip to Kuwait City, and I planned to go on a shopping spree as I had been doing in other Middle East destinations. It was on this trip that I had met Maria and we connected instantly, and found that we were scheduled to fly together on our next trip to Miami. We had been positioned to work together in economy class and surprisingly our Purser was another black woman of African-Caribbean descent. She had been in the game for an age, and she had no further smiles to manifest, even though she was promoted to the Purser supervisor level. Her facial expression blended in with all the other crews faces of despair. The never ending information we had on what we couldn't do in

Kuwait was disheartening particularly for those whose life entailed drinking and more drinking topped up with flirting.

After a six hour flight we arrived in a desert type landscape, and the crew and I disembarked without our regular stash of spirits, lagers and wines and mindful that if anyone had tickled another's fancy on the flight, it would be wise to stay far away from that person. Opposite sexes fraternising in one another's rooms was committing an offence according to the customs of the land.

So far I hadn't met any staff that had caught my eye and mesmerised my mind, neither was I expecting to. But trust Maria who wasn't afraid to tread on egg shells, she was on a mission to flirt and befriend the Pilots. Pilots are appealing men in uniform as the norm would have it, but in my view most pilots were personality- less individuals. I found them too proud and pompous and I had no interest in any of them from any of the crew I travelled with. Still wannabe mistress Maria pursued this cause, trying her best to persuade me to join her even though I wasn't enticed. That conversation between us didn't get the momentum she wanted so eventually she killed it. We did connect on the levels of business talk; Maria wasn't a typical Cabin Crew shopper in designer malls even though she had a tall and slender physique that strutted down the aisles as if she were on catwalk. Her ambition was to use her occupation and opportunity to travel, to become a trader of little gems. Although she was enticed by the fat earnings of the pilots, her goal was to make her own. It was impressive to hear how she had already made contacts with traders in Africa. Maria was dealing in Diamonds and bold enough to travel to zones of conflict in order to secure a deal. She utilised her language skills and ventured into Angola and Mozambique networking and negotiating as the middleman (woman) of various business transactions. Maria was building multiple streams of income from her work and this was inspirational to me, as I had also seen the potential for travel and trade when I applied the position.

Other narrow minded people saw the job as frivolous and flirtatious, and warned me that it wasn't for women who intended to get married. They said a woman who worked as a flight attendant was loose and lost all her respect and dignity. It wasn't just one or two people who expressed these chauvinistic thoughts; it was a whole tribe of them. So I was surprised when *congratulation was in order,* originated from a family friend of the same ethnic background as me. For most of the mind-sets in our community women were to be trained to become domestic goddess in marriage and not gallivanting around in the air and abroad. "This job is for the young, you should be getting married by now." Another relative justified why I shouldn't be doing the job. It was a comment I couldn't get my head around as I believed being a twenty something year old was young. And why should have I been getting married by now, according to whose law? And since when must a man or worst still a woman project onto another the time frame for marriage? The Sex

Discrimination Act 1975 could do with an amendment, a subsection; "as she treats her" in addition to "he treats her less favourably", because often it is our own women that reinforce negative gender roles to each other to maintain the status quo. It is unbearable to have men dictate, and incomprehensible to think women want to add to this, by treating women less favourably because of our low self worth. *Tarts* and *loose* women were the kind of labels attached to female cabin crew by some narrow-minded men. But I was not deterred from pursuing my career as a fly girl. Some viewpoints showed that some people still believed that all women have to get married and that women should abstain from non-marital relationships. Listening to those perspectives would have given me a dose of pre-employment rage on the issue of sexual oppression however I ignored their views and followed my dream.

Once employed, I found that many married women were employed as Cabin Crew staff and travelled with their husbands and that many middle age and mature women worked as cabin crew as it was not a job for only women in their youth. And although it was their prerogative, not all women were in the game of flirting, neither was all the young women bed hopping although there were a few heart breakers, and one such female was amongst our crew on the flight to Kuwait City.

"Next trip I'll be in Australia, might meet someone interesting"

"I guess you must be already tired of Abdul" I replied fascinated at how Kelly found it so easy to move on.

"Abdul has his purposes when I get bored in Riyadh as we all do" with a smile on her face she continued "best advice is to find a rich bloke who can buy your time."

In the midst of our intriguing chats the plump purser hovered around polishing the kettles and giving us cold glimpses as we spoke. We tried to look busy too. She looked so mean I wondered if she knew how to smile and how she came to be employed in the hospitality industry. Kelly went on to let me know about another lover, Femi. Femi her Lagos lover was pretty loaded, had a great sense of humour, treated her like a queen although his family detested seeing her and forbid their blood to marry a blonde vegetarian bimbo. Her story was a reminder of the racial issues from both sides of the fence. Femi's family were akin to a few Nigerian mothers I knew who would fast and pray to prohibit their beloved sons from marrying outside their clan. Yet Kelly was not satisfied with Femi alone, she had meal tickets, many to choose from. But she was far from ready to settle with anyone or find that someone special, her mission was to explore and enjoy. Kelly had men falling head over heals with her and contrary to popular opinion that women are always on a mission to marry, she was a heart breaker.

Kuwait city was calm and deserted; in fact it was built on a dessert plain, so we were surrounded by sand. Arriving in the night, one would think the city was under a curfew as it had a desolate feel to it, except for the lights shining from buildings. I had hoped to see at least a few people walking about, but none whatsoever were spotted as we made way to our lodgings. The new and wide roads were a paradise for learner drivers, where were the cars for road rage? The city appeared modern although traditional styles and constructions still existed.

Despite the warnings, there was an opportunity to go for a hot drink, in the hotel as well as the vicinity around it. I went out along with some male crew and I witnessed liberal Arab women dancing and enjoying themselves. The women gyrated their broad hips to fast paced music in the bars, and danced seductively with men who did not seem to be their husbands. We were able to purchase alcohol as well; the laws must have been somewhat relaxed in specific areas.

The next morning I was awakened very early to a booming call to the city, this was a wakeup call that couldn't be switched off; a call for prayer. The words that echoed were foreign to me although I felt the essence of Islam through an acoustic warning to have discipline. The continuing sounds made it feel like it was fundamental to begin the day in prayer.

Maria and I arranged to meet to go for the tour of Souks, all over the Arab world these open markets where the conventional shopping mode, and barter in buying the 22k yellow gold. We asked other crew members to come along with us to buy or view, however this type of gold was not appreciated by our peers; they found the colour to bright. Maria and I had customers who thought the opposite. The Souks filled up; in each and every store thousands of gold items and jewellery was displayed, and customers were holding conversations in Arabic to get the best deals. Often they would start to speak to us in Arabic and ask us which African country we had travelled from, we responded in English however we didn't give away too much information in order not to be overcharged as *naive British tourists,* who do not know how to haggle for a better price. In such arenas one watching the unending trade it was apparent that Kuwait was an opulent city. Customers were buying gold in bulk as well as perfumery oils, silks and rare expensive cloth. New roads and constructions were also signs of investments in infrastructure and a well to do economy. It appeared that the oil trade brought good returns to the country and its people. The nation however still felt constrained in terms of social movement, it would seem that money was not an issue but liberty was. Whilst I respected the laws of the land and its culture, I became aware that women were hardly seen around, there were groups of them in their native attire in the Souks, but moving around it was apparent the number of women was disproportionate to the number of males in the many shopping arenas we toured.

As Maria and I spent the rest of the day relaxing at the sandy white beaches we noted that wherever we decided to camp we were pestered by Kuwaiti men. It was interesting to engage them in conversation to learn the history and politics of the land, but it always ended in a personal manner. It didn't take long before they would start to flatter us by telling us that we were beautiful and then come into our personal space as they tried to hold our hands or touch our faces. These men must have been breaking the rules by addressing women in public which is frowned upon as it is perceived as a form of sexual harassment. More than once the men mentioned Bob Marley when they saw us, and stated that we were their sisters as we were from the African race. They were in awe of seeing us, a black and mixed race woman, although African women were part of the nation's demographics, but perhaps these were married women or the African women traders, and in us they saw single, liberated women.

At the beginning of the nineties Kuwait suffered from The Gulf War. Following the Iraq invasion of Kuwait, George Bush deployed US troops to combat Saddam Hussein's takeover. I witnessed the aftermath of the invasion a few years on through the stories of the local people. Only men were to be seen out and about, so Maria and I listened to the accounts of the war from the males' perspective. How I wanted to hear the views and experiences from women. After the ceasefire, the UN Security Council was ordered to inspect Iraq's arms, as they were believed to have weapons of mass destruction. The crisis around the invasion of Kuwait and the subsequent fallout of Sadaam Hussein with his neighbours and the west caused instability in the region, added to this was the fluctuation in oil prices.

These factors had an impact on the people of Kuwait. Outside of the men's personal interest in us, they voiced their concerns about their faltering economy and instability in the region in most of our conversations, to a point of tedium for me.

On the return flight Maria and I told our stories to the other crew members, much to the surprise of the other woman who found it hard to accept as true that Middle East men had any incline to be attracted to black women as they believed blondes were favoured globally and especially by Arab men. Kelly was part of the click who believed in blonde goddesses as she practically had a man of colour from all corners of the world. In my view, whatever the case men are men, and regardless of the colour they like the goods that they are hunting for in the end. Men from the Middle East were not an exception. In their case it didn't help matters that their women were prohibited from being in an intimate relationship other than in marriage. It was no wonder the men sought foreign women of any shade. From my experience I understood the sentiments of some crew members when they spoke of the hypocrisy of some Arab girls who when in the West altered their dress and lifestyle to that of the West only to realign again on return to their countries. In such circumstances it is difficult to know if they are principled and strong in their faith or they just comply with dictatorial customs because they have no choice.

The Purser who Maria and I or any other of the crew had not seen throughout our stay listened intensively to our escapades, and we began to see and understand her mannerism. She told Maria and I that the argument she had heard over and over again, was that blonde girls believed they were the most superior in the world and most sought by all men of all colours. As women we waste so much energy with useless battles, women all over the world are created beautifully; the most beautiful are those that blossom internally; true beauty queens. The adage of *beauty lies within* is a simple comprehension. Our Purser also confided in us the hardship she had endured to arrive at that position. She went on to say that the promotion hadn't been easy, she had earned it and it was long overdue after the long service she had dedicated to being a Cabin Crew member. However, she said some girls still belittled her authority. We understood why she had not smiled from the briefing room to the outbound journey. Later we glimpsed a smile as she said she enjoyed flying with us and envied us as Maria and I were fortunate to fly together again on our next trip to Miami, it was rare to fly with a friend.

Arriving back in the U.K I reflected on that journey, it was another good one, the Arabian magic had worked its charms on me, the magical dust penetrated into my mind as I considered relocating there for some years. I did not feel like a minority in terms of ethnicity, many Arabs were black and brown although as a woman being seen as minority was an issue to contemplate. The conservative clothing was not ideal however I wasn't in the habit of wearing revealing clothes, although what I may regard as normal clothing in the overbearing heat might still cause offence in that society. There were benefits of migrating, such as the savings of an expatriate, warm summers, bearable winters and living in a developing and wealthy nation with low crime. I was a fan of the Arab world and henceforth was pleased unlike many of the crew when I was scheduled for one of these routes. At that time the prospects of living there sparkled, in retrospect living a life that could be a lie with all regards to public image and not to my truth was the deterrent.

Flight AUH

I was becoming an expert at gold buying, and seeing Anoushka on the flight to Abu Dhabi I asked if she was up for a shopping trip with me to the Souks, as these outdoor markets sold everything under one blazing sun. I explained to her that not too long before I was in India and was bored out of my head being surrounded by the lifeless crew who had seen it and done it all before or just detested being in India. As we made our way to the hotel, Anoushka and I engaged in deep conversation of a personal level. Both coming from migrant families and being raised in London we shared common experiences. However, Anoushka was not too disturbed by the racial discrimination we experienced at work, she mentioned it but kept referring back to the discrimination of the sexes. For her it was far worse. As I got off the coach and checked into the luxurious five star Hilton Hotel within the surroundings of the spectacular Arabian Gulf, I was heavy hearted. I realised that a feeling of heaviness had settled over me as I absorbed Anoushka's sad personal story. We were so engrossed in conversation I hardly noticed the views of Abu Dhabi city we had just arrived in. She had told me that she was a divorcee with a five year old daughter, and that she was the happiest women on earth to be freed from the ties of a marriage from hell. It had been a nightmare trying to gain her freedom and she had been burnt and scarred to get her freedom. In the first instance she hadn't wanted to be married, but culture dictated the life she had to live, on top of that her husband turned out to be a beast in disguise and his family were all of the same breed. Anoushka said she counted her blessings for being free and able to raise her beautiful daughter who was her joy and pride, nothing else mattered. Her experiences had made her strong.

The bellowing Fajr prayer as well as the rays of sunshine beaming through the blinds onto my face, woke me up. The intense heat knocked me out and the joy of another Middle East trip had made me sleep soundly. It helped that I hadn't indulged in alcoholic beverages which made me merry for a while, but restless and dehydrated later. The Middle East was a destination for detoxification, to slow down the pace and recharge from the more fast past of the Western destinations. The sounds of prayers lasted up until midday. It was the best time to leave for a shopping trip as the sun was not as strong as it became in the mid afternoon. I had learnt from experience that the markets closed for prayers during the afternoon, usually just when I was getting into my stride of shopping. I aimed to buy my shopping in a day, usually the first, as time was of the essence as a crew member. It was wise to tour, shop and treat oneself before taking time to rest before working on the flight home. On this occasion I had decided to depart pretty early so that on return I could soak up the strong sun. I withdrew a few hundred of Dirham from my card and headed for the shuttle bus to take me to the market styled malls. No matter what the exchange rate was, I always managed to get a bargain and it was fun. Apart from trading for gold I had shopping lists from friends and friends of friends who wanted items that were priced lower than in the U.K. The orders ranged from small electric goods, perfumes to Arab weaved quality carpets. I could have become an entrepreneur at that time, if my mind was focused on trading. As I watched the Bedouins in loose tunics covering their bronze skin I felt a strong connection with them as they wandered through the markets, towns and desserts I saw my life in comparison wandering, exploring, and for me looking for a home. I always regarded the demographics of a city to contemplate if I could adjust to living there. From my shopping adventures I noted a few western white women, even fewer black women wearing a Hijab or Abiya, and that men tended to stroll around holding hands with other males.

On return I showed Anoushka my purchases and we delighted in the gold. She of course had compelling stories about gold and how it was used as a way of controlling women. She said it was the culture that rich men bought women with the gold and she suggested all that glittered wasn't gold. Adding further to her feminist campaign she expressed the beauty of living in the western world, the freedom from gender discrimination in comparison to her culture. In all honesty, I understood her viewpoint as I knew of similar stories of men trying to own and buy women from my own cultural background, but I wasn't in the mood to rage about issues of sexual oppression and how it was a global affair, so I kept quiet. From the nation I originally hailed, baby girls and young women were subjected to gender abuse, be it being sold off for marriage as a child, having genitals cut or being denied an education, I was protected by Her Majesty's government and spared because of my life in the United Queendom, although I still was affected by psychological scars of FGM. In 2014, Boko Haram, the militant Islamist group in Nigeria kidnapped over 200 school girls, forbidding them to have Western education with the intention of selling them off into marriage. Today in Northern Nigeria high numbers of girls are subject to female genital mutilation and this practice is also current in other regions of the nation. Anoushka's story was poignant and food for thought; every woman has a story to tell and she was bold enough to share it with me. It was unusual as my regular chats with most female cabin crew centred around standard stories on family and friends or superficial conversations about celebrities.

I spent some time in my sleeveless midi dress, knowing I was safe wearing it in the hotel grounds, I rehydrated by drinking fresh coconut water straight from the large coconut that was sliced across the top, I sucked the liquid furiously from the inserted straw. I who was a lover of heat, was darting in and out of the hotel, I couldn't bask in the sun on the terrace for long, the temperature of 45 degrees Celsius made me take my hat off as instead of it protecting me from the sun it was making me feel hotter. Because of the melanin in my skin, I believed that the sun and I were best of friends and that it would never damage me. I believed skin complications from the sun did not affect people of colour, but over time I learnt to protect my skin as the sun's rays are harmful no matter the colour. On one occasion in these terrains of basking heat a metamorphosis was happening from my feet upwards. Gradually like withered wallpaper my skin was cracking and shedding in layers. It was a shock, never in my life had I ever been burnt in the hot or flaming summers in the U.K. It taught me that the phrase *black don't crack* is simply just a phrase, beneath it all mankind is the same.

Abu Dhabi was an exciting place in 1998. There was a decline in oil prices in the Emirates in the late 90's, so tourism was being promoted and it became big business. Of all the Middle East destinations this was the one that I would be leaving with spicy memories of sun, sand and sea and sad stories about the plight of oppressed women.

Flight TLV

I had always wished to travel to Israel from my earliest childhood memories; the religion I had been raised in subconsciously played a part in my fascination of Jerusalem and Israel. I grew up watching Christian films of Jesus of Nazareth, and his crucifixion replayed in my mind over the years. I was excited to see my roster and schedule to go to Tel Aviv for a couple of days. It was a dream come true being able to go to Jesus' place of death, to unravel the tale of the crucifixion that some believe and others see as fiction. My family being from the South of Nigeria were Christian. The stories in the Bible of Joshua and the Israelites' destroying the walls of Jericho, the Holy City where Christianity was born were captivating to me as a child in Sunday school and so it was my mission to visit these places. So I was geared up to view the city of stone, climb through the ancient remains and meditate. However, the news feed from the Foreign and Commonwealth Office FCO for the safety of the staff was paramount; we were briefed on the risks of travelling into the West Bank. It was during a period when Israel had agreed to hand over Hebron in 1997 and in a resolution of 1998 they surrendered most of the West Bank territory to Palestine after several suicide bombers had killed masses of civilians. Still with the accord in place it was a gradual process for peace and highly risky time to tour, so Bethlehem the birth place of *my saviour* was out of bounds, neither could I travel from Jerusalem to Jericho if I had to heed to the advice. A die hard tenacious spirit that I am, I checked if anyone was willing to venture into other cities in Israel, but no such luck on that occasion.

It was a general view of my work colleagues that the passengers to Tel Aviv are the worst kind of almost all destinations. I quizzed why and what was wrong with the passengers on this route. I was told that they were the most arrogant of all people they had served, so much that their arrogance and manner had made many of the crew members despise the Jewish community. It was hard to believe that they had yet found more nations to feel bigoted towards, and I put it down to misery towards the job and their life rather than anti-Semitism.

The flight was smooth and a short four and a half hour journey, very short for a long haul flight. It was also a job getting used to the Boeing 777, when on most of my trips I flew on the 747, 400 model series. The triple sevens were built to replace the older wide body airliners. They were the first completely computer designed commercial aircrafts. Although it took getting used to it was pleasant to work on this aircraft as they were all relatively new. The flight to Tel Aviv was less work, as other than the usual drinks round there was only one meal to serve plus the normal duty free goods round due to the flight time. During this time I found all passengers pleasant and they were calm contrary to what my colleagues had me expect. What was a surprise to me was the passengers in business class; I had never witnessed Jews with abundant melanin in my life. I had heard of black Jews but had never seen them, and it was astounding to see them in their black attire and black curls as they sat serenely on this flight. On the flight I served men with glossy black locks falling from the sides of their faces, under their wide brimmed hats. I had grown up living near Jewish communities in North London and watched them on Friday evening walk to the synagogues and prepare for Sabbath, these where Ashkenazi communities. These passengers probably were Yemenite Jews, who were originally from Yemen although the majority appeared to have features resembling those of the Beta Israelites from the horn of east Africa. Seeing the various communities of ethnicities that make the one faith of Judaism, and realising that we all are of one sole source, made me feel closer to the passengers on board. It reinforced the idea in my mind that we are all one, in one world.

On arrival in Tel Aviv I was happy to venture about alone, if others wished to stay back and I had to go alone I would, so not to miss out on viewing this sacred land. Had I toured to the ancient city of Jerusalem, I would have loved to meditate, but it wasn't the time for me to do that journey. Instead I wondered around modern shopping malls like Azrieli Centre, and strolled on the sea front of Gordon and Fisherman beaches. I travelled the city widely to appreciate the picturesque surroundings and found something, somewhat of religious nature The Religious Beach, a beach that separates men and women bathers who want to sunbathe in the nude. It was a cosmopolitan and carefree city bursting with a youthful population. Contrary to what I had expected, I was in the heart of vibrancy and modernity, and I was fascinated by my sights. I wanted to feel the history and holiness that I had learnt as a growing child, but I had to accept the change as I saw a thriving western society. I now had a new destination of interest so near to home and yet warm and welcoming. When in Rome do as they do, as I promenaded along the clean sand strips I lunched and dined enjoying Mediterranean Sea delicacies. This was a holy trip: a trip in which I felt whole and happy and warm.

From my room I watched the ambiance and non stop movement of vehicles and tourists below me, there was so much to attract tourists to the town as well as investors, for it is one of the wealthiest cities in the world. It displayed monuments of European as well as Mediterranean design and the elite tended to reside north of the city and the poorer to the South. It was a rainbow of colours from the spectrum of modern outlets to the diverse populations that lived there. The youth population derived from the University they were the party goers that kept the city awake. I wasn't enticed to join in although most twenty something's would like to get up go out and party. I decided that I would return for a sacred and solo journey in another season of my life.

Chapter 5 Asiana

Flight BOM

"Have you been to India before?" I felt like it seemed obvious that I was new, by the question she asked.

"First time."

"Then I shall tell you and warn you beforehand"

I was working in business class on the upper deck and a middle aged, highly articulate lady engaged me in conversation. She became friendlier with me and had more to say to me each time I topped up her tea. Her being a lover of tea, as an Indian lady was normal; however, I sensed that she wanted to pour out her soul, as I poured her tea. I suspect talking about the issues was therapeutic to her. I listened intently to her as she explained the economic and social situation of India; she painted a grim picture which deepened the sympathy I felt towards the people of the country. The Madame was obviously from a well to do background and she felt pity on the majority of the Indian population. They faced morbidity and high mortality due to poverty. She narrated with sorrowful eyes how the divide was despairing between the extremely rich millionaires to the slum dogs' life in Mumbai. I was forewarned that on arrival I would see beggars, lepers, the disabled and others all lined up on the street, helplessly. The passenger gave me a prep talk for the mystical journey I was about to go on; my first stop in Asia.

Disembarking the aircraft and collecting luggage from the carousel was a déjà-vous experience, a time consuming one also! The slow pace at which the queue moved as well as the damp heavy air in the terminal, added to the misery of the lengthy airport experience. Officials in Safari style uniforms didn't attempt to smile as they scrutinized our passports and shouted for the next person in the tropical line of fire. The six feet three Cabin Service Director CSD, looked like he could do with a cold beer to refill his pot belly. He waited patiently to see all crew safely through and then walked with me to our pick up point. The friendly giant complained about India and concluded that I should be glad to be British, indirectly implying that Britain was far superior to third world Countries. In talks about development when focused on which nations were superior it showed the need for maintaining dependency and debtor nations. The corporation motto of one world was not being realised. If the ideal of one love in one world were true it would lose the category first, second and third world.

At the Sheraton I withdrew two thousand rupees expecting to spend it on city tours. I hoped that someone from the crew would be willing to come along even though they all claimed that it was too dangerous to roam about.

Two scrawny porters behaving like Siamese twins brought my luggage up to my room with smiles as wide as they could go, then they hovered about long enough for me to remember to tip them. After I tipped them they didn't budge. I was tired and would've liked to have a nap but they started up a conversation which I found overfriendly. I didn't know if it was the Indian manner. It went from basic chit chat of, *how are you? And how was the flight?* To, *where are you from?* Not satisfied with my answer that I was a Londoner, or British they probed further about my origin, hoping I was an Indian. With my hair at the time chemically straightened to a shiny black, and with their rich melanin skin darker than I was, they hoped we were of the same kin. It was quite unusual to experience that acceptance from an Indian person as my previous experiences with friends and associates within the Asian community, gave me the impression colour was part of a cast system and the lighter the skin colour the higher the ranking in society. So the people with the darkest shade found themselves at the lower end of the social ladder. After I told the two men I was of African heritage, I wondered how high or low they would view me as I was a lighter shade than they were.

My entertainment options were few, having read the hotel tourist guides and information; I settled into bed and watched the television. A few programmes were in English, but there was nothing I had interest in. To my surprise most of the dramas shown featured predominately male actors in the cast, the Hijras. They wore-makeup, and I wondered if they were improvising for women. I watched a sitcom followed by another drama about Hijras' the Indian transgendered society who were born males and lived their lives dressed as women. Through these programmes and a documentary talk show which exposed a lifestyle unfamiliar to me, I had learnt about the culture of the Hijras. I had not seen so many men dress as women, wear more make up than the whole fleet of cabin crew together, and behave in a highly effeminate way. I wondered if they were just acting even though they were reality TV documentaries, but I had to believe what I saw as this was their truth and they had set out to reveal it.

I had to save my rupees for another Indian adventure as none of the crew changed their mind about going out. I would have gone on my own to explore but the CSD said it wasn't wise or safe due to the severe traffic and so I was put off the idea, especially after being told that it was likely that as a foreign woman, I would be touched and grabbed in the streets. During the afternoon I bumped into one of my happier colleagues in the lobby. We had worked together on the inbound journey and become friendly. He said he would come over to my room and say hello a bit later, after I moaned to him that I felt imprisoned and let down. His words were reassuring as he told me to do things alone if I had a strong desire to do something. I believed in that philosophy and that prompted further conversation. Later on he came and knocked on my door all spruced up and I thought we were about to go out to eat or go somewhere of interest. We chatted about everything and anything. More than once he offered to order room service for us but I wished he would suggest we go out. He was of Moroccan origin and talked much about his beloved country where he once lived. It bothered him though that the women were restricted and had to be virgins until marriage and I was learned about other methods and routes couples used to be intimate before marriage. I thought it was a mature conversation but all the talk about sexual relationships must have penetrated into his mind, soul and body as he then pounced on me as if he was a lion ready to kill his prey. I was shocked and horrified. There was no way that I had given him any signals that I liked him in that manner, and I certainly did not see him as anything more than a male cabin crew peer come friend.

"What the hell do you think you are doing?" I snapped at him and pushed him off as he pressed his lips onto mine. In that instant he jumped up and ran out of my room apologising. He left me thinking and questioning myself. *Was I too friendly? Was it sensible for a woman to let a man regarded as a work mate into her room? Was it just part of the package of crew life? How many crew members had told me about the one night stands they had with each other in their travels? Was the lack of sexercise written on my face perhaps a cue to his actions?*

Whatever the case, I felt that his attempt to unleash some Moroccan flavour on me was not a way to express interest to a woman. Yes it was true that we had chatted a lot on the journey in, and yes for sure we hailed from the same continent, and yes we were the only two ethnic minorities on that flight, but hell no did it mean that we had an intimate connection. After I sent him to the door, I felt helpless just for being a woman. I also felt an anger in me rise. Ironically the women were given precautions by the CSD about our vulnerability as foreign women if we went out of the hotel. I was groped in the safe surroundings of the hotel. It was a lesson learnt; not to be naive!

On the return flight he was ever so apologetic, full of regrets for his misconduct, and I forgave him. I felt that I handled the situation very well, being more than a *conquer-ess* by my expression. I listened to chit chat from the crew who complained of runny stomachs and all sorts of pains from the spices of India. The journey didn't have the Indian magic I expected but I left with mega Mumbai memoirs; India however was mystical as I had met my alter ego: the Femme Fatale.

Flight HKG

Despite what time my body clock was on I always tried to adjust to the physical time of the city I landed in. The life of a newly recruited cabin crew member was so exhilarating that no matter how exhausted I was after a long haul flight, I somehow summoned up the energy to experience new things, like a child full of life. By being focused on fulfilling my dream of discovering destinations through my work I was fortunate enough to arrive in the heart of Hong-Kong. Others had missed the opportunity by letting the external negative forces bring their dream to an abrupt end, and I remembered one such person. It was during training that I had re-encountered a young Black British woman whom I knew from a secondary school close to mine. She had been recruited almost the same time as me, and was on the next training group following the group I was in. Her ambitions like me were to travel and meet new people and South Asia was highly placed on her desired routes. We sometimes met during the breaks whilst in training and she would offload her grievances about the corporations' aura, she felt that they were discreetly racist and found it difficult to complain as it was so covert, I agreed. It didn't take long before she threw the towel in and resigned from the training before her first flight. I could have done the same as I had on a few occasions witnessed prejudiced statements and actions, but I bit the bullet and walked on feeling strong yet sad. The sadness was temporary as I overcame the hurdles of induction, intense training and assimilating into the institution, the next step was to sit back and enjoy the journeys, only thing was there was no sitting back, standing for hours on end was more like it.

It was courteous to respect the cultures and laws of the land. No matter how warm it was, it was advisable to wear the Hijab or be fully covered as a woman in the Middle East, although I didn't have to. In Hong Kong the first garment I wore was a Chinese dress, it was fashionable at the time, but I wore it because I was in China. Appearing at the lobby with my striking red fitting dress I caused quite a stir among the senior pilots. *Exotic,* I was called and pivoted to the pedestal amongst a bunch of young European women. At that particular point after about two months of travelling I was radiating my love and light to passengers to crew members and to citizens of the nations I was visiting. Feeling great energy I was rearing to go and had the company of Lucy a young lady from Yorkshire. Lucy was loopy and her flickering blue eyes showed how excited she was. The two of us made a well suited pair of young British women on the rampage, ready to make noise in our jubilation. It was a seven day trip concluding on Christmas Eve, 1997, so we were in high pre-festive spirits. Besides we were still celebrating our new sky high lives.

We hit the town in our merriment, and headed straight to the exchange bureau to confirm that the hotel had given us a good rate of dollars.

"Oh my days, Will," I gasped. What a small world it is I thought as I looked through the glass window. I recognised a former colleague sitting on the other side of the counter at the bureau. A few years back I had applied for the post of a cashier at an International Bureau. I had not the slightest interest in finances, or the banking sector, although I may have ordered that position into my life subconsciously whilst at secondary school. Whilst I was writing my autobiography at school I imagined what occupation I would have in my twenties and at that time the role model women who were in employment outside of cashiers in supermarkets and Marks and Spencer, or in offices were often seen in banks. This is what I wrote as my wish, and it came to pass. I was enticed by the prospect of global travel, and for such reason my energy and passion was noted and I was recruited to the post at the Cheque Point Exchange Bureau. On the job however I lost interest quick. I knew that it would take years before being promoted to branch manager and or be posted to an international destination. But Will had staying power and here he was, the young man who was recruited a little while before me and had trained me. It was good to see him, and he was equally pleased to see me.

"What brings you to Hong-Kong Amanda?"

I introduced him to Lucy and told him that we were newly recruited cabin crew. He told us where the hot spots where and places of interest and bargain shopping. When we left Will, Loopy Lucy told me how lucky I was on international routes; she felt that she stood out with her fair complexion and blonde hair. She said that as she watched Will and I speaking she saw that we blended in with the nationals. I wondered what she meant as Will was of mixed heritage, Black Caribbean and European, and the only thing oriental about me was my red dress.

The first thing we had to adapt our senses to was the smell of the China Sea, as Hong- Kong was on the coast we were inhaling the seas and the Pacific Ocean, natural as it was the smell of raw fish was a shock to the system. The city was on the go and it was obvious that China was the most populous on earth. Hong Kong was part of the British Colony up until that year and other than Chinese there was an elderly white population followed by a working age population of mostly white males. Sign boards and posters were written mainly in Chinese; sometimes there were translations into English. Most other countries I had visited the native language whether dominant or not, there was always a strong use of English. I went through markets and into museums to familiarise myself with the culture and histories of the land. It was a humid atmosphere and my skin felt moist which was beneficial as it was beginning to dehydrate from this new life of life in the air. I went into department stores and all the counters displayed beauty products and had women selling cream most of which read skin lightening. There was an obsession with having the lightest and whitest skin which was evident from the lightening creams sold in markets to the way hagglers waved tubes of cream in my face. They were like pushers on the street corner, trying to sell to skin lightening addicts.

I was a former addict. I was an adolescent with acne, in my late teens the spots turned to post inflammatory pigmentation, blackheads. So I started to bleach these areas, but before long I was rubbing this cream all over my face. Over the years I had listened to brain washed people from the black and Asian communities that felt fairer was *finer*. I had the experience of fading out for a few weeks. Like litmus paper, the acid chemicals changed my colour red for a temporary measure of feeling beautiful. *With a brighter face was I more beautiful*? Beauty truly is skin deep, whether or not I was regarded as beautiful, I needed self-acceptance and looking back it did nothing for my self-esteem. Empowered with knowledge I see how dangerous it was to apply the chemical hydroquinone to my face and the further damage it has to the entire body via the bloodstream. My mind boggles at my folly. My complexion was not a concern to me whilst working at the airline, although at times I believed the whiter skin black women blended in with the majority of the employees. As a flyer there was not a chance I would relapse and buy lightening cream, I loved my brown skin!

The Chinese street marketers became offensive as if I was supposed to apologize for my brown skin. Or maybe there was a mass market of black women and other women of colour with low self esteem buying these products. It was unethical in my opinion to push creams that have no health benefit to anyone into the faces of dark skinned people. The marketers expected buyers to purchase this product to blend in with the ideal colour, white. More recently when I work in health promotion outreach, the public often feel offended when advised on weight loss programmes. They feel that I may have singled them out, although it was random and I was doing my job.

However for health reasons approaching someone who may be overweight is only helpful to the individual. The episode of pushing lightening cream at me I felt was political; it could case rage and spur one on to a race war because it implies there is something wrong with dark skin and being black.

Black is beautiful, the whole rainbow spectrum is beautiful. Beauty is defined firstly as the qualities of a person or thing; also it describes an attractive woman. But the latter is twice in conflict with the first definition, as a person applies to both the sexes and attraction does not sum up all the persons qualities. Women are forced to feel that their attractiveness makes them beautiful, but the second definition alone shows that it is a false concept, constructed to keep women concerned about vanity. I loved wearing red lipstick for the job, it brought wanted and unwanted attention and it did make me feel bright and externally beautiful. I enjoyed wearing make up too, not always as being natural is as fresh as spring, but applying strokes of colour to enhance my eyes creates visual beauty. Beauty is a combination of natural, visual, abstract and auditory, the beautiful thoughts and the sounds of a loving voice also equate to beauty. Meanwhile to maintain the beauty of youth I shopped around for fashionable wears in Hong Kong.

I spotted many familiar chain stores and restaurants like The Body Shop and KFC, but it was an opportunity to try local foods and shops and encounter new and different things. As Christmas was approaching I used the opportunity to buy presents at discounted prices, China was famous for mass production and exporting, and buying from base was economical. There were copies of designer goods, but one would still save by buying original marks.

Lucy and I had been everywhere in the first few days, ticking off all the places of interest, before the mid week back to work schedule. We took a trip to Manila as part of the crew duty, which was a shuttle flight. I was once again celebrated in the Philippians' community, as a bunch of women the cleaners and service staff came on to the plane I became the centre of attention and attraction. It was all positive vibes on this trip and my days went too quick, the week whizzed by as if an invisible fast forward button had been set. I had terrific company, fun times, bargain shopping and a lot of laughs. Sitting at the peak at Tsuen Wan I was thankful for this fly life, here Lucy and I feasted on flavoured pasties for lunch after the cable car trip to the top, viewing skyscrapers of major banks, in scenic surroundings and cool air. That night we had our last supper together eating Shark for the first time, and although it was fried it tasted succulent and light. Seven days of perfection: an old friend seen abroad, a time for reflection of my blessings, it was a trip of a lifetime.

Flight NGO

It was less than a week since I had returned from Hong-Kong, celebrated Christmas and I was off again to spend the New Year Far East in Japan. The schedulers gave us recuperating time from a long haul flight and some days leave when planning itineraries. I was a little prepared for the trip as my training buddy Bella had given me enough brief on the destination when we caught up over the Christmas period. We left on the 30th December, on the shuttle bus to the aircraft, crews' faces were a reflection of mine, despondent. We spoke about our Christmas, most of us had just returned from a trip and were fortunate enough to spend it with family at home, whilst others were not happy to be away but some did enjoy their Christmas abroad. This was a trip to bond with colleagues as we had the New Year to look forward to and bring in the good cheer with one another. Instantly I connected with a crew member and we tried to make the best of the situation working at a time when we'd rather not. She was an experienced member and was not excited about the trip to Nagoya, except that it would boost her salary. We decided we would shop together or rather just window shop as we knew that there were better places for bargains in other nations that sooner than later we would be heading to.

Although we were fully boarded with passengers and we had turbulence on the course of the thirteen hour flight, it was a smooth operation. On a normal day on a westbound flight hyper active children would be up and down from their seats, long queues of passengers would routinely decide to go to the toilettes the instant we started to serve the drinks round. Steering the trolley around the passengers who tried to squeeze down the narrow isle was one of my biggest work stresses. If I could still pour and serve drinks without spilling even when there was turbulence it showed my skills. And if I could do this with a smile on my face without sweating and my make up running, then surely a promotion to Purser was in order. Or at least it proved that I had the skills and ability to fly without wings. On this particular flight, the plane was so shaky that the pilot kept asking passengers to remain in their seats, and these passengers were a good bunch, as they did as they were told. We still had to serve despite the roller coaster effect, and I went on to ask a gentleman who looked sharp from the starched white collars of his shirt to his pinstriped suit, if he wanted tea or coffee. Pouring him his coffee was a task, I couldn't pour it smoothly in one go so I was forced to pour it drip by drip. I timed it well, but, before I handed the black coffee over to put on the table-tray the shakes began again and the cup toppled right onto his lap. Boiling black coffee stained his trousers and must have caused a stinging sensation. I apologised profoundly. Expecting at least an inch of anger for the mess and pain I had caused I was shocked that he didn't blow up. I flustered around grabbing serviettes as I apologised, I was further embarrassed by the fact that I could not dab at the stain as it would be awkward so, instead I offered him serviettes. Perhaps he was practicing Zen and strong meditation techniques to remain calm, as he seemed to view the spill as caffeinated water under the bridge. Furthermore, it was my job to smile, yet he beamed at me whilst I sincerely repeatedly apologised for my clumsiness. I found that generally passengers facilitated my work. If they were calm that calm energy rubbed off onto me. In the same vein passenger's misery transferred onto me as I often absorbed their complaints by showing empathy and putting on a smile. Putting on a superficial smile instigated all the air rage in me, it was so false. On the flight that I spilt coffee on the smart gentleman, the passengers were calm and so was I. Meanwhile, some of my miserable colleagues were still complaining about the passengers on board, and I was sure they were angry about other issues and maintaining their natural tendency to always complain.

For a change I had arrived in a country where the driving was the same side as Britain; I always looked at similarities before noticing differences. The city looked spotless and structured all the hard work after the wars was manifested in the architecture planning. Apart from the look of the municipality I could feel order in the town, in the way the citizens moved, everything seemed methodical. My friend and I went shopping immediately, I picked up a few bits, but it wasn't far different from shopping in New York or other highly fashionable cities, my friend mentioned that they were more Western than Westerners. After getting shopping out of the way I picked up brochures for places of interest as I had a long seven days in the city. Day one was over although it was at least two days that I had been awake after the long flight and arriving in Japan which was eight hours ahead and in daylight so I embraced the new day without going to bed. When I finally got to my bed   I fell into sleep swiftly then at some point I felt as if I was hallucinating, my bed moved left and then right, it shifted forward and backward as if passionate lovers in frenzy were mounted on it, but I was alone and lonely in this city and not the least bit tempted to invite any male colleagues to my room, not after India. Perhaps the *sexpression* idea was ideal to relieve stress and rage and it was why many crew indulged. I dozed off and again experienced movements and shaking, this time beneath my bed, it happened so frequently that I thought that I must be loosing my mind. Perhaps I had worked in turbulence too often on many flights and now I had started to dream or have nightmares about it. Later that night I decided to meet up for a drink with the team instead of sleeping, or trying to all through the night. As the conversations got going I found that I wasn't hallucinating I had experienced a mini earthquake, which happened frequently in Japan. It was a relief to know my first experience of the earth trembling beneath me; it wasn't due to the effects of alcohol. I chilled with the crew including the flight deck team in the bar for a long while before I realised that I disliked many of them there. It had been an evening with pompous and pale pilots who talked about their reckless conquests with women from developing countries for a pittance. Fuelled by alcohol they spoke freely and callously as they guzzled pints and knocked back bottles of spirits. The rest of the crew were of either the same nature or had acclimatised to the kind of self supremacy that was being exhibited. I began to develop a hatred for the institution. Had my African-Caribbean friend from the other training group been right to leave before she even made one trip? Was it worth the fight? I had lost some of my armour. To fight or not to fight? One thing I knew for sure was that I had to focus on what I wanted: fight or flight? It was either that or I turn to the bottle as most did.

I witnessed so many crew turn to comfort drinking, it all started off as a social drink and progressed to over indulgence I discovered as some of us shared our reasons for drinking with each other. The more pints or spirits one was able to knock back the more accepted you became or so I felt. I loved the taste of Baileys, sweet and creamy and brown it went well with me. I did not drink for acceptance, was it rather an addiction to Baileys, or was it an alcohol addiction? Even though at the time I believed that I could handle it. A friend of mine, used similar lines when drinking "I can knock them back, drink the blokes under the table," she bragged. It was interesting watching people drink and transform from polite customer caring smiley people to obsessed sex ravaging beings. It was in the crew room - where clouds of smoke filled the air and the smell of tobacco lingered on clothes long after one retired to ones hotel room - that the true nature of the crew became apparent. It was the space where we dropped the smiles and showed our other side. The drink brought all kinds of behaviours out in people from first class bitching, yes the real cat fights, where it became evident that women have ego's that far outweighed men, it was far from glamorous. It was as if external beauty was ones ticket to heaven and women needed validation to enter. On occasions I would laugh at the way female cabin crew competed for Pilots or big time entrepreneurs. In order to win attention on a night out drinking, the best method was not to excel and shine your own light, but to knock the lights and confidence out of fellow women. *Fake blonde. Not real boobs. She's not that pretty!* was the kind of regular remarks that started the cat fights. The comments were made either behind backs or when alcohol was involved the ugly words were spat out face to face. Craving for attention or the need to feel superior to another woman were signs of low self worth. When these women were recruited psychometric testing would have picked up on positive self esteem, but after some time in service the self esteem would have taken a knock. Cabin crew and alcohol went hand in hand, but the flight deck and alcohol abuse stories I could relay would probably be passed off as fiction.

On the 31st night after getting around in Nagoya with my friend mainly to Buddhist temples and shrines and spending a lot of time in meditation at the Osu Kannon Temple, I happily retreated to the hotel for a rest and to decide what to do for the New Year night. The team had planned a get together, and I had decided against it. There was no way I was to dishonour my dignity by mixing with the chauvinistic and bigoted pilots. I chose the lonely option and wandered around lonely planet. Getting on the train was difficult as I was unable to decipher the native script, not being able to speak at a time when I would have liked to. After only three months of flying the novelty of the job had started to wear off. That particular trip to Japan over the Christmas period had a lot to do with it. I felt that my dream of being a black ambassador of Britain meant I had lost my self respect at times. I did not fit in. At that point I knew that I did not belong and I did not want to just to be able to travel. Before I left home I hoped that I would celebrate the New Year night out with colleagues but it was pointless to jive with people whose lights were out and lived in their own darkness.

Still I had conquered as I returned to the U.K I knew that tough experiences only make one stronger. I was on my own for the New Year and rejected the group because of some of their narrow minds. It was a time I wanted to be with people but I decided to be alone in a totally foreign environment. On the other hand it was remarkable to have been forgiven by a passenger I severely scalded and to have survived an earthquake. I was ready to journey on.

Returning to the U.K I had someone to let it all out on, Bella, her response was to whine over her last trip as well as her problems with her boyfriend. It was great to have someone who was in my shoes, both of us wearing high blue court shoes with sore soles of our feet and sore souls that wept. We had maintained an important relationship since our training by supporting one another. We regularly moaned and motivated each other to continue on in our journey. But what I really needed was therapy, or therapies. I already had the retail therapy of window shopping and spending on bargain designs, I was a shopping addict but I also needed soul therapies. To write would be a healer of my soul. At least I could have been doing something I was passionate about, writing during and after each trip. To release my soul in the words at the end of the day in a notepad; jotting in my journal the beauty and horrors of places new, and chronicling the relationships encountered. All these doings of joy that I let slip by. The benefits of intercourse also are endless, with my new prune wrinkling skin embedded with alcohol a solution to skin treatment could be a passionate night. It would be equal to having a facial. The therapy of sexual love and nourishment was also lost. I was spoilt for choice in creating meaningful relationships. I was meeting men from all walks of life, different faces, and diverse races from places across the globe, yet after a few months in of this work I couldn't remember my last orgasm, tut, tut. I was full of stress and tension and no form of relief. There is always a way to make oneself feel better in any situation and I soon got back to my flow. My jovial self perked up and at the end of the month I was rewarded financially as my pay increased with the high allowances I earned from the strong Yen currency, as well as other lucrative routes I had done in the previous month. I was a flying champion and I was ready for the rest of the world.

Flight KUL

I had a particular fascination with this city and somewhat the South East Asia region, on previous trips I would buy designer garments many of which were fakes but good copies and bag them off to interested parties back in London. I had invited a dear friend that I had known since studying at college as she was an adventurous and fun spirit, and I knew we could re-live our teenage energies on this trip. I had started to get in the habit of packing less and buying more abroad so that I had space to pack items in, travelling lightly has many benefits. On the flight I was excited to have a working holiday away with a livewire: adventurous Angela and my colleagues also liked her. With my cabin bag fairly light too, the crew said I could fill it up with booze galore so that we could get even livelier. Some of the men and particular my purser was expecting an x rated free show from the two of us, allowing his imagination to run wild as he topped up my bag with drinks, I played along and let him continue waffling and fantasising. Angela got an upgrade to business class and was royally taken care of and was offered additional drinks to disembark the aircraft with. It was a great start.

The city with its heterogonous architecture was a marvel to me, combining the influence of Islamic designs, western creations, archaic colonial blueprints as well as avant-garde constructions. The Islamic influence was evident due to the numbers who practised the faith; however it was notable to see Buddhist inspirations too. Malaysia was a diverse make up of religions and cultures which added more spice to its capital. It was a melting pot of the various Asian nations assembling in Kuala Lumpar, a strong Chinese presence, Indians, Sri Lankan's and other Islands off the North Pacific Ocean. Although the nation was Malaysia and Malay people were the majority, it appeared that the influx of Chinese had a strong existence in the Capital. I felt tall amongst the locals with my average height, but shopping wasn't as glorious; the clothes were made to size the nationals, with no consideration for the international population and tourists who may be bigger and taller. I had difficulty trying to find shoes that fitted and kept asking the sales staff to bring adult shoes, and they would say, they were the largest size of adult shoes. Shopping in Suria KLCC mall a glamorous brand new shopping centre with market stall prices could have been fun if I wasn't so big and wide at that time. The mall was located in the PETRONAS Twin Towers, tall glass pillars reaching the sky; they were the tallest buildings in the world. Outside of my cabin crew hobby of shopping, Angela and I were able to go to the tourist attraction parks. As we made our way around asking for directions, the locals who spoke English as a second language went out of their way to be helpful. They responded with a "yes" even if it wasn't a question that required a yes or no answer. Perhaps they were practicing their English as they prepared for the Commonwealth games to be hosted later that year; they were the first to be held in Asia. Many tourists and migrants and traders and expatriates fluxed to Kuala Lumpa as the economy was growing and so it was becoming one of the worlds's most visited cities. I engaged with African Scholars who came to the many Universities in the town, and others who represented their embassy or were on business. The city was a blend of dark skin because other than African migrants, many Malaysians had a deep brown skin tones, and of course skin lightening creams were being pushed so I suspect that some of the lighter skin tones may not have been natural.

I loved the modern urban city juxtaposed with green and natural surroundings on the outskirts. I intended to go on to the Islands for a two day sun sand and sea break away from shopping with Angela and we made a plan to go to the East Coast to the unspoilt beaches. The city was hot and humid so escaping to the coast for clear skies was a treat to look forward too. Then for the first time in all my trips, a circular went around followed up by a phone call to alert us of an emergency meeting. I wondered if something serious had happened as it was odd. We weren't given much time to get ready so I returned to my room and donned my uniform. At the emergency work meeting in the hotel we were informed that major riots had occurred in Jakarta and two other regions. The riots were as a result of an uprising against the new government order. It was just as well I hadn't had a late night the day before as I needed all my strength for the task we had to do. We were taken to the airport where we spent the whole day shuttling distressed passengers who were fleeing the riots, back and forth. The airline put on additional flights to cope with the passengers who needed to be transferred to safe zones. They were of all ages and races; British expatriates, teachers, NGO workers and journalists came on board and relayed their horrific experiences.

It was May 13th, and an unlucky thirteen day it was for victims in Jakarta most of who were the ethnic Chinese communities. It was also unlucky for Angela as she had to spend the day alone at the hotel whilst I worked. At the end of the long day I returned to the hotel too late and too emotionally drained to go out. I explained to Angela how I had spent the day and we hoped the next day would work out better. The next morning there was another wake up call to rescue civilians from violence. Again I had to leave Angie for another day and this time with no estimated time of return. Students had taken to the streets to protest and some had been killed in the process, whilst hundreds of others were severely injured. Properties were damaged from the rocks that crashed into windows, as the students' leashed stones and rocks at the police who shot back. On the 15th May 1998 I was on my third day of rescue team flight crew, it was a moving experience to go through what seemed like a miniature war, to be at the heart of rage. I felt for the families and communities that were subjected to the violence often for no reason of their own. The 16th was my original scheduled day for the short shuttle, as expected, it was another long day and again I returned to the hotel late in the evening. For our hard work and to show appreciation, the CSD organised a banquet dinner for us that night. I always was a lover of the gourmet, the food was succulent, I ate lots of Satay chicken on skewers and my taste buds were tantalized with a buffet of delicacies. We were given a bottle of Champagne for our hard work. Unfortunately for Angela her days were running out as she was returning back to London a couple of days before me. There was no time for the two of us to have an excursion. Had we not utilised our first day trekking together we wouldn't have had any real memories apart from ones of stressed Amanda leaving for the daily rescue mission. Nevertheless, we had our stash of drinks which kept us merry throughout the trip. I regretted the timing although it couldn't be helped, and my friend took comfort in the fact that she was due to take a grand vacation as part of her friend's bridal party to the Maldives in the near future. When she had departed I walked around and I met an international expatriate. For once in my life I relaxed, threw my cares to the wind and I took the opportunity to go out and experience night life in a club with a stranger, it was therapeutic.

Flight DMK

I was feeling relaxed, all the tensions had disappeared, the wrath of the passengers washed over me, the insincere smiles had suddenly dispersed, perhaps I was just getting used to the job. I had done almost one year service with the airline and my annual leave was due. I was also due a well deserved vacation which I decided to take in the great company of my sister. The Far East was enticing so Julie and I decided to go to Thailand for our grand summer holiday. It was so unwinding being able to go on an aircraft especially for a long haul flight and not think of checking for safety, monitoring galleys and customer service. It was my time to unwind, although it was my second nature to do the checks. As the staff went through their procedures I was discreetly doing the same, it was a loyal thing to do, and they were my colleagues. There were several reasons for choosing to retreat to Thailand; one was the weather, the other was that it was tropical and exotic, and it was a great for shopping! Wearing designer clothes didn't do much for me; I found that it only gave me a short term ego boost. However shopping wasn't entirely for me but for the business woman I had become. It wasn't only clothes, bags and shoes I planned on hunting for but for electronic products, a few techno savvy friends (it was the 90s and not everyone had PCs) had asked for laptops. We arrived at Don Mueang airport, the nation's former international airport in Bangkok. It was large, modern and welcoming. It was also one of the world's oldest international airports and Asia's oldest airport.

Bangkok was hot but not in an overbearing way. The drive through the greenery had a therapeutic effect on me. We meandered through shrubs and lengthy palm trees in the tropical rainforest listening to the sounds from the woods before the driver entertained us with his meditative music. Short bursts of hot rain came down then dried up instantly. Taking in the surroundings was so relaxing. A few buildings, some express roads, and people casually cycling in their straw hats, it was nature at its finest. I enjoyed that moment and I felt as if the world had stopped for me to appreciate true beauty. I was for once able to be, not do, just be in the moment and feel life. It was one of those rare opportunities where I was in the moment and not too busy in my business to enjoy the moment, as was usually the case.

As we mingled in the chaotic traffic the relaxation period was over and we were welcomed to the commotion of street life of the congested Bangkok city. The roads were heavy with various forms of transport ranging from heavy duty tankers, motor vehicles, four wheel drives to manpowered cycles and cycling carriages. The first thing we did when we got to the hotel was use the gym and spa as we felt energised. We didn't take long as we didn't want to miss out of any of the outdoor life. However, after our shower as we were just exiting our hotel we were enticed to try some cocktails; we couldn't resist the spirits with cream and crushed ice; turquoise and blue laced liquors and toppings of citrus fruit. In the heat we drank and drank and drank trying various concoctions. It made us more the merrier as we entered the vibrancy of street life. Our first explorations took us to the Vimanmek Museum and Mansion - the largest in the world. We then went to the shopping malls of several floors and outlets, using the Touk Touk traditional method of transport. It was enough indoor activities for us as we both felt that the city was a place to enjoy the outdoor life because of the good weather. From then on we ventured into several markets as there were markets in abundance, each with their own speciality; flower market, Chinese medicine, fruits and vegetables, home and electronic gadgets among others. The same night we tried the Elephant mode of transport and we travelled through the dim lit roads that were full of the electric energy from vendors and shoppers. Stepping up on to the bowed elephant before it rose was a humbling experience, a connection with other inhabitants of the earth. It felt majestic, to perch high on an elephant's back and move slowly and grandiosely through the night in an urban atmosphere.

Each and every day there were new things to explore for cultural interest as well as places to retreat to for relaxation. Market hopping took a major amount of our time as there was so much to see. Many of the markets catered for cook outs, try and buy and eat on the go and the air was filled with the aroma of hot oil and fried pastries. Shopping was unending due to the thousands of vendors everywhere and it was not possible to cover all the markets and all the tourist attractions. As we went around spending it was uncomfortable to witness many people in tattered clothes around us or loitering around the hotel asking for change, hands stretched out displaying grime embedded fingernails. We needed some tranquillity so we decided to take some relaxation time to chill at the Pattaya beach resort away from busy Bangkok.

In Pattaya the locals were friendly as were the people in Bangkok although that's the way one has to be in order to sell, but on the exotic island the people seemed to have a genuine interest in us. We were young black women whereas most tourists and migrants were of European descent and so our uniqueness sparked up many conversations and admiration. We also admired the lovely Islanders and for a moment I thought how I would have loved to migrate to the peaceful and natural surroundings. The fun of the retreat was the speed boat as our driver took us on an unforgettable journey. We were tossed up and down and sent bumping and crashing through the waves, at high speed. After which we ate fresh fish and vegetables and watched the locals by the sea surrounded with green hills. An old fisherwoman in native dress was busy selling fresh fish and we saw young lady boys with long blonde wigs and massive shoulders, they where everywhere. As some of these cross dressers were close to me I noticed that they had flawless skin that a woman would die for. Their makeup was applied to perfection but their massive manly hands and coarse voices were a give away. The trans-genders walking around selling their bodies was the norm for daytime activity, the sex trade was on the open market.

The beach escapade was healing and the entire Thailand experience was refreshing as I was surrounded by natural unspoilt environment. I appreciated the beauty of trees in contrast to built up malls. To live in this type of environment was to be free from fashion labels draped on mannequins enticing a twenty something to buy me and wear me. This relaxed natural environment away from the fast paced city life was truly a more civilized way of living. Our last days were spent rushing around trying to do everything from collecting gems, purchasing jewellery and meeting manufacturers. African women traders in their Ankara wears were busy doing this too, although they looked young; they seemed like veterans in the trade. As time was of the essence we decided to utilise it well and so we stayed out to the wee hours of the morning and participated in the night market. It was a little more hectic than day time, we attracted a surge in attention but we were able to ward the onlookers off. Since we had done the night markets, seen the red light district we decided to top it off by touching base with the night life as we had met some people from the international community who had told us where the hot dance spots were. It was only a sneak view, although it was enough as we were weary from a full action packed holiday.

On our last day we went to recover and to meditate at the temple, the home of Buddha. Through travels my mind was open to other cultures and religions despite that it is written that to worship another God is to be in conflict with my God. My truth is that whichever method you try and communicate with your source, whatever path you take, there is only one destination: LOVE. In my fly life a message that resonates well with me from Buddha is; you are your own master; things depend upon you. I had mastered my dreams of flying and had accomplished my adventures in Asia.

Asia was both exciting and taxing. It was testing to be amidst extreme poverty and wealth side by side and interesting to experience the continents contrast between modernisation and traditional traits. Furthermore I had learnt that race was not just about black on white, but Asians had serious complexes on dark skin perspective issues. From India to Thailand the transgender community was on the surface, unlike other parts of the world. All the same, my love for the continent of Asia is eternal as are the memories.

Chapter 6 Africana

Flight JNB-DUR

My first trip to Africa with the airline was to the unfathomable nation of South Africa. This grand continent was spiritual and strong and from the North to the South it was blessed with abundance of minerals, sacred ancestral tales and above all a blend of peoples with beautiful customs and traits. Naturally enthusiasm took hold of me on this spiritual journey, and as I flew over the Sahara and looked out of the window pane the scenery was breath-taking. On the African soil, my colleague Sonia who had worked in first class waited for me to disembark the aircraft so that she could walk with me and show me the way. As we walked she made the point that we should be proud as we stand on our territory.

Sonia a tall and beautiful stewardess had been in the job for a lengthy period and was even more in minority when she was recruited as she was one of the earliest African-Caribbean women to join the airline. But she had stood her ground despite her experiences of being isolated and excluded from the mainstream women because of her rich brown skin. Her confidence was a threat to some staff as they had expected her to fade away into the background but instead she blossomed beautifully and enjoyed her work even if she was in solitude. And so I did feel proud to be in Africa again, home of my ancestors although not a home I had any familiarisation with having been born and raised in the Diaspora. Here were brothers and sisters in my home continent but in heterogeneous houses of languages and cultures. I felt the same vibe as Sonia; our spirits had connected in this environment. We took a short coach ride through rich red soil to the hotel and when we arrived I was at full peak as the sunshine had awakened me as I captured the life in the city of Johannesburg. I was fully recharged despite the twelve hour flight. The hotel was situated in a pleasant suburban residence. I dropped my belongings and took a shower, allowing the tepid water to massage the knots in my back, before heading off into town with Sonia. The first thing she wanted to do was to braid her hair for a price that was next to nothing compared with what we paid in London. I accompanied her to her regular salon where the staff was like her neighbours, as soon as they saw her they started catching up from the last time they met, a few weeks before. Sonia filled her friends in with follow up stories about people in her life and told jokes over bottles of Fanta. It was not long before I was motivated to do my hair, and a couple of hours later we stepped out into Jo'burg rocking the latest braids styles. We trekked around a little as Sonia guided me to places I could go to over the next week, so I noted the local malls and spots to eat at. Just as in West Africa, people gathered outside and socialised under the sun, it was interesting to see the vibrant outdoor life that seemed more popular than walking around in shopping malls.

Later in the afternoon Sonia and I ate alfresco then we were joined by friends of hers. She told them about life in the U.K and the Midlands where she came from and in return they relayed stories of their lives and communities. As the conversation carried on the topics got more intense from telling personal tales to talking politics. It was great to be engaging with real people, talking and learning and not merely going shopping and taking tourist photo shots. As we socialised I observed the behaviour of the locals many of whom had joined us in the afternoon to drink or were already stoned. The young men downed four to five extra large cans of brew per hour on average. They drank, they danced, they talked politics and danced some more, and were merry in their stories of hope and despair. A regular friend of Sonia got carried away and said he was delighted to see that she had for once travelled with a black female colleague. He became excited and outspoken and in the process revealed his perspective of sexuality and racial hatred.

"That's better, you normally come with gay men in your company, those whiteys" he said berating our peers and indicating through his gestures his interest in me. Sonia didn't for one instant tolerate his being homophobic and retorted that they (South Africans) had their own political issues to deal with instead of slanting homosexuals. The debate moved on to black oppression. From the discussion it was difficult to make sense of their new liberties as they had been mentally chained to segregation and subordination for years, policies were renewed but mind-sets seemed to have stayed the same. Sonia became angry with the mind-sets of the locals and she let out her vexation. We were two young black women heatedly debating Afrocentricism on my first day in South Africa. Eventually we left the party and journeyed back to the hotel talking of Kwame Nkrumah, Marcus Garvey, Pan Africanism and Independence movements. It was a newly post apartheid era and Mandela's administration had been in office for only one term, the complexities of the nation's history were beyond our perspectives of an immediate; *say it loud I'm black and proud*. The damage of apartheid was embedded in the majority of the population. It had long term consequences such as crime and poverty, and this resulted in high morbidity. I had only been on the ground in Johannesburg for a few hours and I witnessed the after effects of apartheid. The trip was an awakening to the harsh realities of the atrocities inflicted on the continent of Africa. On my first night I reflected and although I enjoyed being in Africa; there was a sense of grieving and rage within me.

A few days into the week I went along with a group of my colleagues to the Soweto and Safari tour, which took us into the townships where the majority of the black population struggled to survive in abject poverty. Shacks as homes sprawled across unlevelled ground congested together not far from the exquisite

Safari inspired hotel decor where we lodged. The living hell juxtaposed against the heavenly diamond life stood out like black against white. The crew were silent; we all were silent as we listened to the histories of the political events and horrors that were experienced in Soweto. This was a nightmare that extended to living daylight as I saw the aftermath of the ancient and contemporary war of South Africa. It was the battles that drove people to new locations, and led them to arrive in masses in the city during the Second World War only to live in slums. It was the battles based on greed where the British and the Dutch together and at times in opposition created the union of South Africa and created a haven of heaven for themselves. As we drove out of the slums and into deserted land for the safari the nightmare was behind me but for my brothers and sisters it continues. Sitting in the jeep in the jungle watching the wild animals with binoculars the reality of survival of the fittest came to my mind and I realised that that man and beast were not very different.

Safari sightseeing was a chilling and exciting experience. We trespassed into the jungle animal kingdom. I had the wonderful company of a male steward who was an experienced Safari trekker, and had done this and several other similar trips so I would ask him to go into detail or repeat words I had missed by our native Safari guide. He was the adventurous type and would repeat activities and excursions over and over again in the same country; his philosophy was that everyday something new happens and we receive different experiences. His lacklustre wife was the complete opposite, she had accompanied him on this trip as they were travel companions on most flights, but she would rather stay in the hotel. On that day and most of the week I enjoyed his company as we went around the city together; when we ate he advised me on the best roasted bush meat to eat and the drinks to try.

After the safari we stopped to chat and enjoy the weather. In that space I was detached from the miseries of the disadvantaged communities. All that I had recently witnessed had escaped me. Like a movie, I had moved from one scene to another. I was in a happy scene of a multi-racial group of indigenous South African tour guides, myself and the European Cabin Crew, and we had just left the other scene of sadness and segregation and oppression. It crossed my mind that if I could, I would capture and freeze a happy moment and transport it to places where the pictures are not so bright so that light would shine there as well.

My next stop was Durban, a modern conurbation, diverse with African, Asian and European races, many of the crew spent their time enjoying at the beach and topping their suntans. Sonia and I decided not to lounge on the beach for long. She used the time to meditate from all the anger she felt in South Africa. We returned to our hotel and had to unwind, no matter how many times Sonia had visited South Africa previously there was always a divine connection and movement that stirred within, I also felt it. In the evening we decided to party hard as aboriginal South African's did, so that we could free our wounded spirit. For the first time I went to a hotel club with the crew and drank hard like the locals, booze was cheap, the dance music stirring and the effeminate male crew really knew how to boogie, and they were great company. Intoxicated to an abysmal degree I was no different to the liquor loving bothers on the streets I had met on my first day in Johannesburg or to most of my cabin crew colleagues who drank to their hearts content when they landed at their destinations.

As we left the lodge and returned back to the airport a comment resonated with me from a colleague sitting nearby as schoolchildren ran after our bus waving as the dust blew into their faces, "happy and humble." And that was the spirit of Africa, a place of dancing and joy despite sorrows and hardships, and a continent of opportunities for growth. If I could live like that; happy and humble and inspired to grow then there would be hope at all times. On the return flight to London a young white South African passenger had an overwhelming interest in me, not quite believing that there were two of us on board, having seen Sonia in the first class cabin he thought he was seeing double, we had the same hair do, but we could barely pass as identical twins, Sonia was a lot taller than I. Perhaps the white South African man was learning from the embracing British and was keen to make a friend in a black woman. He kept on monopolising me for chats whilst I had lots of work to do. That Soweto tour served as a lesson for me. I witnessed the horrible history of blacks being oppressed by the white minority immigrants in South Africa. It was heart-breaking, yet I was still able to love and serve and smile wholeheartedly in my duties to all beings on board. It was my higher self - and it was this light that connected to the light in the enthusiastic passenger. "As we let our own light shine, we unconsciously give other people the permission to do the same." Nelson Mandela 1994.

Flight CAI

As I ventured to different locations, it was as if I was looking for truth. Travelling to this destination afforded me the revelations of the origin of civilisation that is credited to the ancient people of the land. I arrived on the mysterious plateau feeling surreal and hazy. It was probably partly due to the trip from our hotel to the city centre. Our driver had flown us to the Giza municipal, as he aggressively sped through Cairo city, I was unable to observe the surroundings due to the bumps and jolts and crash landings I had as my head hit the steel framings of the withered vehicle. Increasing dust and sand from the Sahara winds hit the windscreens as we progressed unapologetically through the stream of traffic. The pollution of the largest African and Middle Eastern city added to the discomfort and it was amazing that we arrived in one piece. My colleagues and I were relieved and grateful to arrive at our destination and to breathe a breath of fresh desert air once we exited the car.

Our first stop and focus of interest was to see the Pyramids to discover the history of the tombs of the Egyptian Kings and understand the period of Pharaohs. The trek was an adventurous assault course, trudging through the sands on foot for half the way before we journeyed the rest of the crossing on the backs of camels. Riding on a camel's back felt majestic. The hard hike became a serene traverse as the sun's rays blessed me on the slow camel ride; in the horizon I saw one of the great wonders of the world and it was awesome. It was a natural terrain as locals also took their donkeys for walks across the plain. Their days consisted of being hospitable to tourists, like us with a reassuring smile on their face, this time I had the privilege of being a passenger. As we approached the central place of serenity, space closed in because although it was pretty early in the day there was an overflow of tourists like us ready to witness the ancient technology of Egypt. It was amazing that people from across the world had gathered here, being drawn to the pyramids as if they were places of worship. Although they were not temples, it was the Shrines of the Pharaohs that were captivating. We learnt that they built these tombs for reasons varying from maintaining their bodies in the mummies, maintaining their possessions and also to maintain their souls in the tomb. They had succeeded in maintaining their spirit to be worshipped as people were drawn towards these sites magnetically, thus indicating the soul never dies. The expedition to the pyramids left me with grand inquisition, how were they built? How were they maintained over thousands of years? I was astounded by the shape of the cones pointing towards the skies as a symbol of worship of the sun God Ra, and perhaps the pyramids were temples as it seemed that people flocked from all over the world drawn by the spirituality of the place. It was remarkable to see the corpses in bondage, and I marvelled at how the tombstones were preserved despite erosion. Seeing The Great Sphinx created a lot of questions and I thought of the power of the Pharaohs, the strength of lions ruling the land and the guarding of treasures. I also had to spare a thought for souls departed the labourers who toiled under the sun for future generations to view; they were a pedigree of strong men.

After the amazing tour the rest of the time was spent haggling in the market place, as tourists do. We bartered the prices right down in order to get a bargain. The markets had silk scarves, oils and perfumes which were good gifts. I was given further discounts than my Caucasian peers, it happened during our desert tour and on almost all our ventures; perhaps the Arabs remembered their Nubian brothers and original inhabitants of Egypt. It was amazing to visit the mysterious monuments and to be in this grand nation, a nation of ancient history that relates to all humanity; from the Nile Delta to the Niger Delta came my ancestors, from the Nubian Kingdoms to Roman and Greek empires the history of Egypt, ancient Kemet spans far and wide. The British also had their stake in the land as a British protectorate, until the Egyptian Revolution in 1952 it was a British territory.

On my last visit to Egypt on a mission to the mountain of Mount Sinai I felt vulnerable, as I took the risk of travelling alone as a woman. The guides took a strong liking to me and I by no means felt flattered. They talked about me and made it obvious even though they were not speaking English. At the end of the all night trek up on top of the mountain, I was shivering as I was drenched in sweat despite the cold altitude, then a guide caught my gaze and held it there for a lengthy moment with his stony eyes. He told me that I would not return to England. It was a beautiful mountain meditation except for that incident. Imagine; he thought no negotiations were necessary. He wanted to trade me for camels and keep me in the mountain because of my origin. I didn't even have a voice, it was as simple as we've seen this beautiful Nubian woman, and we want her here in the mountains. At such moments I realised the significance of the rights I had as a citizen of a country that respected women's rights. The guides actions made me feel as if I had no rights. I was enraged at the apparent existing unequal and unhealthy gender relationships. Even if he didn't carry out his threat, the audacity of the guide to think he could lay down the law on me. Nevertheless, the Egyptian expeditions all were wake up calls to face my fears, seek for truth and honour my inner voice.

Flight LOS

Oh bloody hell, not a LOS, I am doing a sick, the usual crew reporting off sick when scheduled for routes to the developing world, in particular, Lagos. There were the exceptional popular African hotspots at the time, such as; Abuja, Accra and Lusaka. Abuja was described as clean, calm and modern and poles apart from its sister city of Lagos where the congestion and crime put fear in the staff. Accra was a place where many crew enjoyed the beach life namely Labadi Beach as a favourite and the crew loved the temperament of the friendly locals. Lusaka had a combination of elements both Abuja and Accra offered, it was rapidly developing and recommended for feeling safe in the friendly city with lots of interesting activities. Crew spoke fondly about their exciting visits to the world's largest waterfall at Mosi-oa-Tunya/ Victoria Falls as well as having visited game reserves. However, for certain destinations in particular Lagos the crew didn't have a good word to say about the city. The passenger's overloaded hand luggage which cabin crew had to force into the overhead lockers causing the female crew members nail's to snap in the process gave staff more reason to complain. I had become nonchalant of who the crew liked and disliked by then, but all the complaints about Lagos and Nigerians- too many-made me label the employees as Naijaphobic.

I should have known that if one is on a standby shift the only likely destination one will fly to is Lagos, Nigeria. So I was going to my motherland again, this time not fully prepared but ready for the venture. How prepared I needed to be depended on the nature of the trip. If it was a family visit, then I was definitely under packed. *"Whey ting you dey bring for me from jand?"* was the initial welcome I got from family and friends back then in 1995 when I first visited Nigeria to visit family. When I landed in Lagos, the first time I felt awakened as I stepped on African soil. It was an unforgettable visit during the time of military rule. This time I was on a business trip with a few night stops, hardly enough time to see relatives and impossible to supply every ones needs. Being in the western hemisphere did not mean that I was wealthier than my family back home, contrary to widely held perceptions; in fact, often it could be vice versa. When I received the call that I was going to Nigeria I was delighted. My work was taking me back to my roots. It was exciting because it would bring back the memories of my first trip a few years back, it was exciting because it was my country, having dual nationality had benefits, and it was also exciting because a year earlier the nation had started its transformation to a democracy which meant abundant opportunities for growth.

In the briefing room we were advised on the current concerns of the city, no go areas and to keep in groups on excursions. Despite being told not to leave the hotel under any circumstances, for me, it went in one ear and out of the other. I was determined to go on a Lagos rampage, there was so much to see and do in this over populated African city that I loved. I was surprised to see two other black crew members in the briefing room; it was somewhat unusual to have a total of three of us on one flight. The three of us bonded instantly and the soul sister and I knew we would link up for the evening meal and drink in the crew room. On the outbound journey we gained adoring attention from other male staff, she was supposed to look like one celebrity and I another, and we laughed about it. I guess being ethnic minorities we were unique, and for some crew members from far away villages and shires it was a first or a rarity to speak to dark skinned people, be it positive or negative. *Exotic* was the name usually associated with us, by the men of course, and especially the pilots. I read between the lines which meaning of exotic they referred to depending on the pilot's admiration or depreciation. On this trip it was nice to be able to have hair conversations amongst other topics, with my *sister*.

"Bite your tongue, I don't ever mention my roots" she said as we chatted in the galley after serving dinner in economy class, she wanted to save me the humiliation of mockery if the crew knew   my origin. I found it absurd! It was more than absurd and I found it a shame to hear my colleague voice this. I felt that she believed the origins of ethnic minorities should be concealed in order to avoid ridicule or in order to accommodate attitudes and other people's perception. She must have felt that up in the air and in our world the minorities were subjected to ignorant and offensive remarks about their countries of origin in the workplace. The irony of it was that I could see her point; many times in life I wanted to become a wall flower in conversations about my heritage. Sometimes I sheepishly laughed along with the perpetrators' who thought they were being funny by making ethnic jokes and at other times I cursed under my breath, but I never challenged ignorance from gang culture or from individuals who made slighting remarks discreetly. It was as if I had a rock on my shoulder. But I understood where my *sister's bite your tongue*, comment came from.

In 1965 the first Race Relations Act was implemented in Britain; however it was ineffective over many years in outlawing discrimination in the workplace. When my colleague made her remark it was during the period the Race Relations Amendment Act 2000 made institutional racism unlawful. More than half a century on and we were still jumping over hurdles of intolerance of black people in the U.K. The post war migration after 1945 saw hundreds of Caribbean migrants settle and contribute to rebuilding Britain in labour and fiscal contributions, during a time when racism was rife. One remarkable woman named Claudia Jones became an activist for human rights to empower minorities and created a celebration against discrimination by introducing the Notting hill Carnival in 1959. Jones was a heroine, a true flyer, not only did she stand up for her rights and that of her community, she left a legacy of flying colours and flags as we celebrate the carnival annually. Despite the presence of blacks in the UK for seven decades (in reference to black presence since post war history), we still faced marginalisation in employment in the private and public sector and my colleague's expression showed that she was experiencing it firsthand.

I was on top of the world on arrival; no matter what the circumstances or experiences I would face it was the joy of being in the nation of my yearning through spiritual and ancestral connections. I sat amongst the leery crew for once on this particular trip at the back of the coach, a change from sitting somewhere in the middle and alone looking out the window. Some were already guzzling down their beer; the more elegant drank wine as we made way from the airport into the town of Ikeja. In the short ride I gazed onto the lively streets where real life scenarios played themselves like scenes in the movies. I had emphatically made my plans for city trekking over the next few days.

"No Amanda, you will stand out like a sore thumb" one crew member advised, followed by another. There was truth in their comments about getting lost in Lagos as I had not lived there. I had history in this country and I was not subdued about it, and I told my peers stories about the first time I came.

"Are you going to go like the locals in their flip-flops, and carry your gear on your head?" The slurs started. That particular comment was much milder than when once someone labelled Nigerians uncivilized. Somehow, I was so used to this, in reference to negativity towards Nigerians, that it had made no difference being in the country than when I heard such remarks on other flights. Nigerians were not solely targeted, if it wasn't towards Nigerians, Arabian's or Israeli's it would be targeted at the Chinese or Indians. I built immunity to the colour and culture bashing from the authentic Britons. To loose my sensitivity meant that I had lost my dignity. Wearing my uniform with pride was a paradox; as I also lost my pride when I absorbed abusive comments directed at my people without reacting. As I listened to ignorance and became numbed by their words and behaviours it was clear that I had changed from an energetic woman to a depressive over the years.

In the evening the three of us of darker shades were the only representatives of the crew that met downstairs for dinner and drinks. This was unusual because most trips I had worked on the crew religiously met for a drink, or a few until morphing into drunk and disorderly characters. Crew rooms were always full, the alcohol abundant with cluttered tins and uncapped bottles of beer on all tables. Transferring from long flights of recycled oxygen to rooms which were foggy with smoke, it made no difference about the lack of air because crew felt obliged to meet for a drink. Lagos must have been petrifying for them despite being lodged in a secure five star hotel. Perhaps in their darkest dreams and hallucinations under the influence they had foreseen that kidnapping of foreigners in Nigeria was to come in the approaching decade. A tour guide had been allocated to us from the hotel, he had made the threesome turn into a group of four at the bar. He was fascinated with my soul sister colleague and so he hung around way after his work hours.

"You are as beautiful as the women in the horn of Africa" He said. At first it was cute, then the flattery turned increasingly clichéd, and her appreciation wore off. She thought he was after something; it must have been the *Las Gidi* hustling she often heard about. Some Nigerians had a reputation of hassling, many others made their way and progressed the generic way, but all Lagosians had skills to survive. Before we departed for bed the tour guide arranged an itinerary for the following day to take the crew for an excursion to the stadium, the crew had been allowed out of their ivory towers and I was overjoyed.

As I made my way to my room, I became convinced that I could actually stay in the hotel for the next few days like a hostage if the trip was cancelled as there was great sightseeing for me around the hotel. I had spotted one or two eye candies, I admired their solid calves and body draped in national colour kits.

"Hey..., footballers on the loose." Like a giggling girly I called my friend in her room to let her know what she had been missing, she was excited too. I had never been a fan of football, neither on any of my trips over the years had I been on the prowl. That night I wanted to have fun just like I knew this trip would be and these national players where an arm's length away. I had never seen myself as an African WAG, but either way I was drawn to their fitness wearing green and white or the opposition in green and yellow, here was a reason why woman like me like men in uniform. Just as I was entertaining the idea of going to seek out the football players the lights went out. I found myself engulfed in blackness; the chance and mood to put on my glad rags and seek an adventure came to an abrupt end. It was the official welcome to power challenged Nigeria. Perhaps someone watching over me disapproved of my intentions and had blown the whistle and shown me the red card. Game was over, it was time to sleep.

I woke up feeling euphoric; I had a good night's sleep and there wasn't a need to detox, as I had abstained from alcohol. By midmorning the pickup time for the trip to Surele Stadium was set. I had hoped for some kind of activity, I was not being defiant towards the safety and guidance from the Cabin Service Director but I knew that no danger was awaiting me. The turnout was fairly good; we had almost a full coach of eager crew wanting to experience Lagos life or the football experience in Nigeria. There was so much hype about football in this country; if it wasn't premiership league matches being religiously watched, it was national tournaments driving them crazy.

A few years prior I had watched Nigeria play a friendly against England in my hometown of Wembley. The atmosphere was electric, never had I witnessed Nigerians – apparently the happiest people on earth - so joyful than in the stadium. Of course I had experienced the hearty laughter and extreme generous hospitality of beverage buying on tap, at many Nigerian events, but when it came to football, it was as if heaven had opened its door and showered laughter to each and every Nigerian in the stadium. Not a frown upon any face as Nigerian fans made their way to their seats in optimism. The crowds eagerly discussed the way the game would go. In the heart of winter with jeans and t-shirts, green and white scarf's, hats and Super Eagle shirts, there was unity. Regardless of whether from North or South Nigeria everyone in green and white sang their hearts out for their country. One song after another of cheerful chants and comical choruses, the ambience was enough entertainment that I didn't feel the need to watch the football. Yet, as the players dribbled the ball and the crowd sang "teach them to play" I was steadily indoctrinated into the game. I jumped into the air and waved my hands like a ranting referee as the match went on.

From that U.K match experience I knew what to expect in terms of watching the game in Lagos, however I had never anticipated such a turn out. It seemed as though all the houses had emptied out into the street. Millions of people the youth, middle aged, elderly and people with disabilities lined the streets and roads of Lagos; it was truly a national support. Growing up in Wembley, I had never witnessed this level of love from English fans for their national team. The road was filled with streams of cars, yellow overloaded buses and little bodies squeezed through the congested traffic as they sold bananas, cut oranges and water to anyone who had their window open. The pavements were heaving with bodies back to back with some being carried shoulder high; they waited, sang, danced and celebrated before the match began.

It was an atmosphere of a carnival without the floats, or any screen for spectators to watch, yet people waited happily.

It was a day trip indeed to cruise at zero miles an hour on the Ikorodu Express Rd into Lagos mainland. Far from being an express trip we were entertained by a fellow black British cabin crew male, who wanted to pass the time doing caricatures of Nigerian faces he saw by the roadside. From time in memoriam, blacks had always entertained Caucasians in song, music and dance, but the sixties civil rights movements fought against the disparaging racial stereotypes of the Blackface theatre and media, however this colleague in his subjugated thinking felt the need to stand in front of the coach and mimic his brothers on the street as he pulled faces and exaggerated his full negro lips. As I experienced suffering and built immunity to racial slurs he too must have lost his soul. Perhaps he never had the soul connection, as Black British children of the same generation we grew up and watched shows like The Black and White Minstrel Show. This must have been his way to fit in and please the majority. Still it was a new millennium and to continue that behaviour was a disgrace. Embarrassed of our colleagues Mr Caricature behaviour, the soul sister began to express her black pride as she told me to be proud of my country, contradicting what she said to me on the inbound flight.

As we approached the stadium the hustlers were more abundant, they banged on the coach window. Many were begging, others hurled insults as they pointed and commented on the white faces in the coach. At this point the crew members wanted to justify their nationality and political perspective. As the match was between Nigeria and South Africa, it was assumed that our coach was carrying white South African fans and us the few blacks in the coach were presumed to be original South Africans. It was evident that post apartheid resentment was still held.

"No we are from England" a discourse had started through the open window between an inquiring young Nigerian, and the male crew member who added that we were in support of Nigeria not South Africa. This conversation motivated the tour guide to get my final answer, he already knew my roots and we had talked about my previous travel here, but now he wanted to know if I was loyal to the British or Nigerians, highlighting the example of the English born former premier league footballer Efan Ekoku who chose to play for Nigeria his nation of origin. It was because I was part of British Airways that he thought that I was devoted to Britain. He had no idea that in England when they played the friendly against Nigeria I sat on the Nigerian side, even though England was my adopted motherland. This is because I am not exclusively British but multi-cultural in this equation, British with a prefix, exotic. At the time of purchasing the ticket for the England verses Nigeria match the English sales women asked if I was buying tickets for the England seating side. Far too often and from both nations I have been questioned as to who I am faithful to. My kind of patriotism is amorphous; I refuse to be restricted to belonging within the borders of a nation.

As we disembarked the bus there was a great jostle, the guide and security held back the surge of the crowd. The people closed in and hovered around in hope; as if the crew of whites were missionaries ready to resave Africa and empty their wallets. Some men swarmed in on us, they were mostly touts. A couple of them were more persistent and managed to break through the security cordon. One of them, who from his faded kaftan and the colourful embroidery kufi cap, I could tell was from the north, shoved his tray of paraphernalia in my ribs and flashed an orange stained teeth smile at me. "*Madam, see fine things o, any colour sha,*" he waved a batch of folded white handkerchiefs in my face. I shook my head and as we were bundled away, still insistent on any sale he then called after me that he could change Naira at a good rate. "*Abeg, I give you good price na!*" In a short while we were in the stadium. The elite of Nigeria could easily afford their tickets, whilst the majority of the nation's population apparently still struggled to *survive on less than a dollar a day*. No matter how deep they worshipped football, they gave their support by cheering on the streets instead as they couldn't afford to spend their hustled earnings on a privy match. Inside the stadium, the young ladies sported designer clothes, and the men donned their casual club collections. Trendy and carefree they were the new nation of youth to experience the democratic rule. Whilst me and the soul sister admired the male fans and ignored the game, Mr

Caricature had spontaneously decided on getting married in Nigeria, he gave his undivided attention to the female fans rather than footy.

With a 2-0 win, Nigerians were happy, the crowd partied till the night and we arrived back to the hotel feeling the spirit of the nation, happiness. I was extremely happy for the freedom to enjoy Lagos and fulfil my intentions. If for the rest of the time there was nothing to do I was satisfied. However, I made calls to the few family members I had who resided in Lagos and to the others in Port Harcourt. It was impossible for a re-union with any member of my family. I was unable to connect with them and that was a disappointment, but I was in my element to be in Nigeria, the source of my ancestors and the nation in which I had an estranged or secret love affair with. To be in exile did not mean that my passion had died, absence made my heart grow stronger.

On the return journey there was a callout mentioning my name. The ground staff rushed into the aircraft pacing down searching for Epe. I meanwhile was in the galley chatting with the team and preparing for take-off. All of us where alarmed, he had located me and said "they told me Epe was here," looking down at the names on the sheet. *What have I done now? I hope I am not going to hold the aircraft up!* He became all smiles, "you are Epe, Amanda, I saw your name on the sheet and I had to come and meet you, YOU ARE BRILLIANT, you are a Nigerian?" He simply wanted to meet me, and was elated to see a Nigerian name as staff. It was a relief and we all found it a funny and interesting episode watching this man run down looking for an Epe.

I was aware that this flight would be manic, but I also heard, although the news was too late that one of my sports idols was on board. I was rejuvenated and this hadn't happened on any other of my previous trips, now I see it as saving the best until last. I had the opportunity of working in business class on return but I stuck with being at the back in economy, and what a mistake I made. A colleague told me that John Fashanu an ex English premier league footballer was upstairs in business class, and for me there was a correlation between the word WAG and Fashuna, but it was too late to change back to business class, I had made my decision.

As usual the flights to and from Lagos were full and the passengers were very demanding. I had learnt during training that Nigeria was the most lucrative route of all British Airways flights, and business class cabins always sold out. I was not surprised at Nigerian's spending power, and I saw how the duty free trolleys were consumed instantly, this was the norm. It was not the selling of duty free that bothered me, but the constant gesturing of hands by passengers who needed attending to. Most passengers had the tendency of haughtily calling the crew as they would similarly do to their *houseboy* and *housegirl* at home. Their attitude was as if they saw us as insubordinates.

As I sipped my apple juice in the galley in the little free moment that I had, I became a counsellor cabin crew; it was no surprise that this passenger got up and out of his seat to come and, pour out his soul to me. Throughout my strides up and down the isle he smiled with a sense of familiarity. I gathered from his accent and different manner that he was not a Nigerian and he informed me that he was from another West African state and was on a new venture to gain asylum from the U.K having been deported from another European Union State. He bent over and leaned over the drinks bar as he relayed his story to me. It was his calmness that moved me, particularly because he told me about the humiliation he faced being handcuffed and led onto the aircraft of another carrier. He was marched against his will whilst passers by in the airport and passengers on board gawped at him like he was a hardcore criminal. In the event of his protest he suffered a small seizure which resulted in him being in a more relaxed state and then he was easily bundled onto the plane. I listened silently with a sympathetic face without interrupting. I thought about the anxiety he must have felt having to go through the same ordeal all over again. This time he was entering the European territory to plead for right of abode on humanitarian grounds. On hearing his story I understood why he was going to try again. In his homeland members of his family lost their lives in conflict and some were injured and disabled. He had corresponded with two members of his community who were refugees in London and they informed him of the process for him to try his luck. I guessed he chose me to speak to because he related to me in terms of my skin colour and was fascinated to see my colleagues and I working on this flight. I was unable to offer any suggestions on immigration procedures or reassure him of being accepted into the country. My wearing the uniform gave him the impression of oneness and inclusion in the institution and one with her majesty's government as a whole. I was reminded through that conversation that not all travels are for vacations, or family visits or shopping sprees or business travel. Unfortunately, some people are mobile not by choice but travel due to medical conditions or to escape death and in search of life elsewhere. For some it was a dream to escape poverty, abuse and war and I was humbled on hearing that passenger's story. It made me count my blessings for the safe surroundings I had known.

There was no need to pinch myself as I did when I first started, dreams became realities and I had travelled far and wide and connected. I had completed my mission and it was time to move on. The soul sister had squinted her eyes and looked puzzled when she asked me what I would do, after I told her that I intended on leaving on the return flight. It was that flight, my last flight of labour, my return to motherland that was my awakening to follow new dreams. I only had a slight inclination and responded that I would do youth work, all I knew was that I had had enough. It was an exciting time as I headed back to another mother land, the last time representing as Black Ambassador; it was time to prepare for a different kind of take-off. The thought of having to return my gold credit card which I used to shop on my scintillating trips all over the world was worrying, I wondered if I was making the right decision. No more jet setting. I was giving up a life and career many people envied. I knew that I would have some regrets. The reality was that despite all the negativity I had been through, if I had to live my life again, there was no question that I would be a Fly girl again. If only for a while.

I starting off as a simple recruit sipping tea then I regressed to toxic and strong beverages; my lifestyle changed drastically, as did my body. My mind opened to new ideas from the multitude of visits to the East and going into the wilderness in the West, and all other destinations in between. I was inexperienced and naive on the first flight to America and the myths and superficialities were more exposed. By the time of my last flight in my final African adventure I had become a tough cookie.

Chapter 7 Arrival

I took off and landed safely as the Divine mother earth has always protected and guided me in my journeys. Most importantly I am grateful for the health I had to do my job. Before commencing work as a cabin crew member, one undergoes a vigorous health screening. I had to be strong in spirit, body and mind; one has to be fit to fly. Landing after my last flight, I reflected on all the travels and travails of a fly girl. My dream, spurred on by reading books such as Gulliver's Travels and Around the World in Eighty Days as a teenager, had been accomplished. I had had my shot at global adventures and it had been a worthwhile experience. For in this experience in addition to the pursuit of pleasure I had learnt more about myself in relation to others around me, understood new perspectives on racial attitudes and altitudes of rage as well as the fear and the power of a sexual being. I relished the pleasurable moments of those astonishing times; it was like a spring bath, fresh and bursting full of minerals. I drank from this fountain and I am grateful.

As thousands of stunning woman lined up and competed to try the jet set life, it was not about being pretty, rather about being persistent and passionate about life and people and engaging in our world. My natural traits being a lover of fun and friendly were the simplest assets to have as the work meant meeting new people on each and every trip, so one needed to be social or learn to be so. Touring from the America's to Asia was an enjoyable experience, what with the fun of meeting new friends on the job and overseas, making the world that slight bit smaller than my regular family, neighbours and local community to a global community. I had shared spaces with people of different races and religions and we blended harmoniously for the most of the time. It was an awakening to open my mind to other religious behaviours in different lands and experience how others live. I had to shut down my concepts and accept alternative lifestyles in the free world. This made me like a child ready to experience new things on each and every flight. It was challenging adjusting my intake of food, in the USA I overate with their large portions, whilst in Asia particularly Malaysia I was in disbelief when room service arrived. Checking into my room after long flights I was expectant when ordering an appetizing rice filling meal. When I saw it I was sure they were trying to put me on a regime. The mould of rice from a bowl sat sparsely on my plate, easily to be eaten in three mouthfuls. I was used to a plateful, circumference filled and still rising with rice. Our family, relatives and friends didn't do portion control when it came to soul food, and Sunday dinners of rice, plantain and chicken. It also was a challenge to walk past liquor when I left this job. The bar in my apartment when I was crew was stocked with various strong beverages. On my days off I invited friends over to indulge in my homemade cocktails. If they were not invited, they would still head over to the pub, my house. I hadn't grown up in a home with alcohol storage, we only drank on occasions. When I look back to that life as I advise clients in my work on the alcohol guidelines and limits, I see how damaging my lifestyle was. I never drank by safe units of the daily recommended allowance, but that sort of behaviour is not limited to the life of crew it can happen in all work cultures if one does not have control of their mind. Equally strong willed people will not over drink in the fly life either.

I was astounded to be appreciated as a black beauty in different parts of the world which revealed to me my subconscious low self esteem, as a result of the negative connotations of growing up an ethnic minority in Britain. This shed light on to my race narrative and the expectation of others to exclude when it was clearly not the case, however, this stemmed from a common culture thread that was systematic in my work environment. I can relate with a pilot, Senior Captain Doug Maughan who talks about the casual racism in the institution, and exposes the depth of racism amongst his peers of middle age pilots and who particularly target blacks and Asians. In 2008, he said, "racism is prevalent now in BA" in his conversation about institutional racism. On reflection, I can add my perspective to his comment that individuals need to look into their own personal institution on race, yes starting with the man in the mirror. BA justifies themselves as being an equal opportunities employer and has policies on discrimination. Still in improving equality BA would do well to employ masculine women (muscles are a criteria for this work) as they do feminine men, and make it optional for women to wear make up. BA has an international crew team and now has increased numbers of multi-racial staff. Crew I have met have friends and relationships from different races, yet the racism was apparent and felt in the airline. However, I see Britain as a nation that adopts other cultures and absorbs foreign nations into the fabric of the nation, and for that it is linked to being named Great. It has open embracing arms through policies, except that, at times people from minorities do not feel welcome in institutions, or the country at large. Racial discrimination was also experienced by me whilst travelling around Asia when traders would push skin lightening creams to me in the markets, their preference for lighter skin tones could be deemed as racism. The notion of racism is very shallow, as so is discriminating based on the colours of ones hair or the colour of one's eyes. When we become enlightened and uplifted to see beyond colour and regard our fellow beings as equals, then the altitude of rage will fall. "Until the colour of a man's skin is of no more significance than the colour of his eyes- Me say war" Bob Marley 1976. In travels I noticed it is not only black verses white but opposition within people of one colour, the ethnic and national differences are the discrimination demons facing the black community in the continent and the Diaspora nations. When we elevate and fly we are able to see past our differences and unite as one family of the human race. How do we not judge a book by its face? But when we interconnect and bond in spiritual relationships we adhere with nature.

As I walked the skies I met beautiful people of one race and although we were not homogenous we were an extended family, yet at times we react negatively towards each other due to global issues of economic, racial and social injustices. In this unhealthy environment we build toxins and like aeroplanes we send out our negative emissions into the atmosphere. In my travels and the basic conversations with passengers or meeting people all over, we have this thread in common, venting out our concerns on injustice. It may not change the world but it is a step forward to talk about disparity as it affects our fellow beings and perhaps talking can effect our future actions. I believe that when I discuss issues I am working from a higher level and it helps to release a lot of rage in assessing the negatives aspects in my life. The still small voice was my ultimate help, a soothing voice in times of sadness; its whisper and guidance to safety to a scared woman in strange places. The voice from a high arena took care of the fly often vulnerable woman. As I look back to my flying days and I reflect on platonic and sexual relationships there is much to learn from. I am grateful for my rights as a woman, as I have witnessed other women who are not free.

I was blessed to meet my dear friend Bella, a friend in my time of need and a true friend indeed. Coincidently we threw the towel in at the same time and we found out that we had both quit a few months after we left. Bella had always complained of loneliness on the job as did many other crew members. After a few months the joy of travelling in a rush for business was not so exciting for both of us. But for me I felt the loneliness they spoke of in addition to feeling isolated and angry. I had planned on doing this work for a few years, so to resign after almost completing three years was a success. It was my intention to travel just to write and so by this book the whole dream has been accomplished. World renowned author Sonia Choquette in her book *The Power of Your Spirit* talks about her days as working as airline crew, she enjoyed the benefits of travel and meeting new people but felt that she was not using her gifts the way she had wanted to. I resonate with her feelings as I was aiming to write during my employment, but I was not in the right frame of mind to write and therefore knew that I had to move on. I moved on to work with young people it was another calling and I was employed as a Learning Support Assistant in an inner city secondary school of special measures. Friends and family were shocked of my decision; some horrified and thought I was crazy. Including my motherly personal manager at BA, who asked "what on earth will you do next?" Many people thought there was no life beyond BA Cabin Crew. My father was in disbelief, thinking I was a quitter and relayed to me his story about unemployment due to racial discrimination in the 1960's, but my sisters understood. People did not believe that having been fortunate enough to be employed to travel the world by a top airline; I would throw it all away, just like that. And they all asked the predictable monotonous question, "why did you leave?" Staff in the school I worked in after I quit BA thought the same, and for some time when the rowdy teenagers screamed, fought and showed behavioural problems, I for a moment missed planes and flying. But the decision was personal and I question them; is it a job for life? My time was up and I knew I would not fly eternally.

In hindsight I reflect on the privileges I have experienced as a Fly Girl, it was a combination of trials and tribulations as well as a treat to tour the world for a living. After the clouds empty its waters, the roses begin to blossom, these words was my personal mantra in my troubles. But on a regular day I could be soaking in the sun, sifting sand dunes or at serene seas and scenes of mountains, blessed. In the right company the possibilities were endless, activities ranging from go karting, quad biking to hiking and snorkelling. I am grateful to have had the many perks granted to airline staff, and to have rolled on the red carpet with celebrities on a regular day, as I met and conversed with several television personalities and others known in their fields, and meeting my brother and basket-ballers in Boston. My family had the benefits of receiving ninety per cent off flights and further discounts on hotels. It was a lucid dream, with a few toss and turns: I encountered riots and became part of a national rescue squad, face to face with racial and religious conflict up in the air and championed sexual harassment, and stood standing or sleeping as the earth shook beneath me. I was lost in my self and finding new ideas and identities, my beliefs fluid; as well as getting lost in strange notorious territories and returning unscathed. I had to wake up from the dream and face my reality; it was my choice to be grounded. Before I got into a catastrophe that I felt was brewing, it was time to set sail and change direction, and wave a heartily goodbye to planes. The uniform that I took pride in was the hardest thing to give up although I was relieved when I returned them all. I was going to miss the elite life of lodging in plush hotels, and after I left at times I wished I still had that life. As I resigned I was sure of one thing: I was free, my wings were unclipped and I had completed my mission.

Although we live best in the moment, I recall and learn from the challenges I surmounted and can use those lessons today to reach new heights. We don't have to be equipped with wings like an angel to fly, but especially during turbulence to have faith in ourselves and then to take action; to believe in our goals is taking one step each day until we reach the top of mountains and soar to the skies as eagles, always remembering we are so fly.

Customs

In this epilogue I state attributes I believe are customary to maintaining A Fly Girl persona. The travel bug never stops, the love of meeting new people is a lifetime affair, and opportunities to reach new destinations are within our reach only sometimes we are blinded to them or too ungrateful to receive chances to move from one place to a higher level. To clear customs I must pay for dutiable goods, I must pay my duties as nothing in this life is free, except the air we breathe. I must pay through my service and sincerity to it and the universe will respond gratefully. Whilst on earth in order to fly it is my custom to:

1. Love myself by listening to my inner voice.

2. Love myself by being my self help coach, self motivator before I seek external support.

3. Look after my mind, body and soul.

4. Lead the way by following my own path.

5. Appreciate my unique conception.

6. Stand alone to stand true to self.

7. Practice, practice and practice.

8. Persist until the end.

9. Fail and fall, feel the fear and get up again.

10. Arise and rise to my highest self and prepare to take off.

Author's Note

This story has been hidden in my archive for over a decade. There is a time in life for everything and it was perfect timing for me to write this story. I knew that I would write about my travels one day and I was naturally inspired to flow freely under no pressure, at the time I chose to do so. The joy of writing this book can be compared to some of the greatest moments I had in travelling, incredible. As a memoirist I was initially writing for myself to monitor the changes in my life and my thinking, as well as how society and nations concepts change over time. I also thought about the responsibility I have as an author to present my story with accuracy to facts and events that happened during my travels.

As I scribed my story and gathered information the process then turned into a creative and research writing project. I spoke to several others who were and some still are in the position of Cabin Crew to hear their views and to compare and contrast. I have come to conclude that we all have different experiences and there are many tales not just one representation of an exotic British Airways crew member. It is vital for writers to express eloquently and not be misunderstood. It was therefore essential and I was fortunate to have a trusted friend Ellen to read, clarify and adjust the points that I had written after my first draft, her attention to detail and professionalism in giving feedback have been lessons in writing.

I have learnt from writing the story, that I am also responsible to be the author of my life. I, like all of us on earth have had experiences of joy and pain through this life. In my encounters from travelling and working with BA I either could feel up or down depending on external occurrences. Regardless of what is happening on the outside as the creator in my life I must feel victorious and not victimised. It was the creation in my mind to travel and to write that encouraged and enabled me to be a fly girl. It is also the drama in my mind that makes me feel defeated when I carry excess baggage of previous disheartening experiences. I believe it is a challenging task to empty our load but it is best to travel light in order to encounter the treasures this life has to offer.

Acknowledgements

Thanks to the Epe family first and foremost for their belief in me particularly my father who called me a writer from earliest days; my siblings and my sister Julie for her hypnotising words that stopped me procrastinating and starting the book writing process. My parents love and tremendous support enabled the creation of A Fly Girl. I appreciate the critical engagement and time taken out from my first readers who reviewed this book Barrister Charlotte Proudman, Author/Coach Lillian Ogbogoh and Author/Journalist Vanessa Walters. I am also grateful for the continuous coaching in goal setting from author Winsome Duncan. Special thanks go to my writing buddy author Ellen Banda-Aaku for her consultancy and first draft editing service. Sam Wall has been a great muse, collaborating cover ideas and I am indebted for her kind considerate generosity. I will always cherish the old Brent Town Hall Library, Forty Lane, Wembley where I grew up to love books. Last but not least I thank all those who have been participants in my research and all the friends I made during my life in the air. The Creator made this possible.

About the author

Amanda Epe is a British born London based author. She is interested in writing, education and international travel and has a Masters in Education, Health Promotion and International Development from London University. *A Fly Girl* is her debut book; her prior creative writing has been published in several anthologies.

A member of UN Women UK her mission is empowering women.

www.msroseblossom.org

Publication History
"I am" in *Brown Eyes*, 2005
"Afro Britons" in *Brown Eyes*, 2005
"The Diaspora" in *Brown Eyes*, 2005
"Brighter Days for African Beauty" in *Hair Power Skin Revolution*, 2010
"Seri" in *The Strand Book of International Poets*, 2010

"Criminals at the Creeks" in *The Strand Book of International Poets*, 2010
"Descendants of a Missionary" in *Saraba Literary quarterly magazine* 2010
"I'm Guilty on three counts" in *Mr Wrong*, 2014
"How Do I Love Me Like a Rose" in *7 Shades of Love*, 2014
"How Do I Love Thee Haikus" in *7 Shades of Love*, 2014
"The Dream Catcher" in *Born For This*, 2015

"Life is a journey, in which we are all travellers."

Amanda Epe

Lightning Source UK Ltd.
Milton Keynes UK
UKOW06f0608160317
296772UK00018B/512/P

9 781849 145589